JOURNAL FOR THE STUDY OF THE OLD TESTAMENT
SUPPLEMENT SERIES
234

Editors
David J.A. Clines
Philip R. Davies

Executive Editor
John Jarick

Editorial Board
Robert P. Carroll, Richard J. Coggins, Alan Cooper, J. Cheryl Exum,
John Goldingay, Robert P. Gordon, Norman K. Gottwald,
Andrew D.H. Mayes, Carol Meyers, Patrick D. Miller

Sheffield Academic Press

Sex, Honor, and Power
in the Deuteronomistic History

Ken Stone

Journal for the Study of the Old Testament
Supplement Series 234

In Memory of
Lori Jo Roberts

Published by Sheffield Academic Press Ltd
Mansion House
19 Kingfield Road
Sheffield S11 9AS
England

Printed on acid-free paper in Great Britain
by Bookcraft Ltd
Midsomer Norton, Bath

British Library Cataloguing in Publication Data

A catalogue record for this book is available
from the British Library

ISBN 1-85075-640-6

CONTENTS

ACKNOWLEDGMENTS

This project was completed with the assistance and support of many individuals. In a slightly different form it was accepted as a dissertation at Vanderbilt University. Thus, I would like to thank Douglas A. Knight, my dissertation advisor, who encouraged my ideas and coached my efforts from the beginning. I also thank the other members of my out-standing committee, James Barr, Renita J. Weems, Amy-Jill Levine, Mary Ann Tolbert, and Susan Ford Wiltshire, each of whom gave me important advice along the way.

At a crucial point I was given the opportunity to present a portion of my research to the AAR/SBL/ASOR Constructs of Ancient History and Religion Group. A version of that presentation, which helped me to begin the formulation of several of the ideas presented here, appeared as 'Sexual Practice and the Structure of Prestige: The Case of the Disputed Concubines', in E.H. Lovering (ed.), *Society of Biblical Literature 1993 Seminar Papers* (Atlanta: Scholars Press, 1993). For making that oppor-tunity possible, encouraging my research, and providing valuable feed-back, I thank James Flanagan, Paula McNutt, Claudia Camp, David Gunn, and, once again, Douglas Knight and Renita Weems.

Several individuals helped me in more personal ways. Willa Mathis Johnson, friend and colleague, was always willing (and continues to be willing) to give advice and a sympathetic ear. My parents, Drs H. Lynn and Mary Ruth Stone, supported my educational endeavors for years, even when they led in unexpected directions. Without their support, I would never have reached this point. Finally, I thank Dr Horace L. Griffin, who assisted me in many ways, great and small, while I worked on this project; and who, with Sheba, gave me a space within which to labor.

I dedicate this study to the memory of one of my oldest and dearest friends and one of my first readers, Lori Jo Roberts.

ABBREVIATIONS

AB	Anchor Bible
AOS	American Oriental Series
BDB	F. Brown, S.R. Driver and C.A. Briggs, *Hebrew and English Lexicon of the Old Testament*
BHS	*Biblia hebraica stuttgartensia*
BTB	*Biblical Theology Bulletin*
CBQ	*Catholic Biblical Quarterly*
FRLANT	Forschungen zur Religion und Literatur des Alten und Neuen Testaments
JBL	*Journal of Biblical Literature*
JQR	*Jewish Quarterly Review*
JSOT	*Journal for the Study of the Old Testament*
JSOTSup	*Journal for the Study of the Old Testament*, Supplement Series
JSS	*Journal of Semitic Studies*
OTG	Old Testament Guides
OTL	Old Testament Library
RelSRev	*Religious Studies Review*
SBLMS	SBL Monograph Series
TDOT	G.J. Botterweck and H. Ringgren (eds.), *Theological Dictionary of the Old Testament*
VT	*Vetus Testamentum*
VTSup	*Vetus Testamentum*, Supplements

Chapter 1

SEX, CULTURE, AND BIBLICAL NARRATIVE

Introduction

References to sexual activity can elicit a wide range of reactions. Depending on the form which they take and the context in which they are found, representations of sexual contact may cause excitement, disgust, amusement, fear, curiosity, and a host of other complex and often contradictory feelings. It is no surprise, then, that speakers and writers make use of sexual rhetoric. Politicians, journalists, novelists, religious leaders, and scriptwriters have all learned that language about sexual activity, in various forms, is able to produce effects upon and reactions from an audience. Sex is a powerful symbol, and the successful rhetorician learns to manipulate it.[1]

The use of sexual imagery is by no means a modern phenomenon, however. On the contrary, there is ample evidence that representations of sexual phenomena have a long and complex history. Erotic art, for example, has survived from various cultures of the past, and erotic paintings found on pieces of pottery have served as evidence for stimulating new interpretations of ancient Greece (see, for example, Dover

---

1. A terminological difficulty surrounds the word 'sex', which is used in contemporary English to refer to two distinct (if related) objects: the differentiation between male and female, on the one hand, and sexual activity (as in the colloquial phrase 'having sex'), on the other. The term 'sex' as used in the title of the present discussion refers primarily to the latter object, while the former is discussed below in relation to the term 'gender'. However, the term 'biological sex' is occasionally used below in instances where it seems necessary to distinguish between questions of anatomy ('biological sex') and the cultural interpretation given to such questions ('gender'). The latter differentiation is a common one in gender studies (see, for example, Rubin 1975; Ortner and Whitehead 1981), though some of the presuppositions upon which it rests are beginning to be called into question (see, for example, Butler 1990; 1993).

1989; Keuls 1985). Sexual imagery has been used in written discourse as well. Ancient thinkers as influential as Plato utilized language about sexual relationships in the construction of philosophical arguments (see Halperin 1990: 113-51). Examples of erotic poetry have also been recovered from a number of different cultures (see, for example, Pope 1977: 54-89; Lichtheim 1976: 181-93). In addition, the representation of sexual activity has played an important role in storytelling. People tell, and apparently have always told, stories about sex.

It is obvious even to the casual reader that references to sexual activity appear in the Hebrew Bible as well. The biblical legal discourse includes a variety of laws and admonitions which attempt to regulate various types of sexual contact (see Frymer-Kensky 1989; 1992: 187-98; Eilberg-Schwartz 1990: 141-94). The Song of Songs is one of the most famous pieces of erotic poetry ever written, and debates about its inter-pretation have often centered on the question of whether the book's meaning ought to be based on a literal or metaphorical reading of its sexual imagery (see Pope 1977: 89-229; Falk 1982: 62-79; Brenner 1989: 67-77). The prophets of Israel, as cognizant as any modern politi-cian of the power of sexual rhetoric, sometimes used metaphors of a sexual sort to communicate their religious messages (see Bird 1989; Weems 1989; 1995; Frymer-Kensky 1992: 144-52; Yee 1992). There are also a number of stories within the Hebrew Bible in which sexual activity of one sort or another figures in the plot. Genesis, Ruth, and Esther, for example, all contain elements, sometimes significant and sometimes less so, to which the term 'sexual' might be applied.[2]

The focus of this project is on the narrative books referred to vari-ously as the 'Former Prophets', the 'historical literature', or, among many Hebrew Bible scholars, the 'Deuteronomistic History'. This body of literature, encompassing the books of Joshua, Judges, Samuel and Kings, contains within its heterogeneous material a number of stories and episodes in which sexual activity plays a role. These sexual elements are inextricably intertwined with information about wars, religion, and politics, information that has been the focus of academic investigation much more frequently than have sexual matters. To be sure, the sexual aspects of these stories have been pointed out and commented upon in

---

2.   For an examination of some of these narratives, see Bailey 1995. Bailey focuses upon a different set of texts and a different set of ideological assumptions than does the present study. However, his examination of the link between ideologies of sexuality and ideologies of ethnicity opens up an important area for future research.

the massive amount of material that has been written on the individual passages in which they occur. Yet these same aspects have only rarely been the starting point for academic inquiry.

It is argued below that references to sexual activity in the Deuteronomistic History, in spite of their differences, betray a number of similarities to one another. It is also emphasized that the narratives in which these references occur were produced in a society quite removed from our own in terms of cultural worldview, and that our understanding of these narratives will increase if the differences between the cultural assumptions underlying them and our own cultural assumptions are taken into account. A sustained focus upon the uses of sex in biblical storytelling, and upon the presuppositions which such uses entail, might help us to recognize aspects of the cultural matrix out of which the biblical texts emerged, aspects which have not always been emphasized. Thus, not only does the Hebrew Bible speak about sex; an examination of biblical representations of sexual activity may tell us quite a bit about the Hebrew Bible and about the network of cultural and symbolic meanings which it presupposes.

The chief goal of this project, then, is to consider some of the possible interrelations between cultural notions about sexual activity and the structure of certain narratives embedded within the Deuteronomistic History. It is argued that these narratives are structured in relationship to cultural assumptions about sexual activity that involve the quest by males for public honor, power, and prestige. One's status as a sexual subject is seen to play a crucial (albeit complicated) role in this quest, though differently for men than for women. A reading which takes such cultural presuppositions explicitly into account will be offered as a more plausible interpretation of the significance these stories may have had in the ancient world than interpretations which read the stories from the perspective of modern Western moral and cultural codes. An anthropological framework and a narratological method, discussed in Chapters 2 and 3, will be utilized in order to develop such a reading in Chapter 4.

Sex and Biblical Interpretation

Although sexual matters are only occasionally the explicit focus of Hebrew Bible studies, readers have had to account for instances of sexual rhetoric when dealing with texts in which they occur. There are no doubt a number of factors apart from the structures of the texts themselves that have impacted this history of interpretation. For example, one could consider the influence of religious institutions, generally conservative on sexual matters, upon readers of the biblical texts. One could also consider the widely held assumption that there exists a 'Judeo-Christian tradition' of sexual ethics which can be differentiated clearly from other traditions and which has existed with only minor modifications from the Iron Age to the present. Biblical scholars have on the whole probably been more aware than many of their contemporaries of some of the ways in which this assumption needs to be modified.[3] Nevertheless, it would be unwise to assume that biblical scholarship has remained entirely free from popular misconceptions about the continuity between biblical perspectives on sexual matters and beliefs about sexual activity that appear among later Jewish and Christian communities. Sir Kenneth Dover commented several years ago, in the preface to his study of Greek homosexuality, that there may be 'no topic in classical studies on which a scholar's normal ability to perceive differences and draw inferences is so easily impaired' (Dover 1989: vii). While Dover refers to homosexuality in particular rather than sexual practice in general, it is perhaps safe to assume that such difficulties are, if anything, even more severe in the case of the Hebrew Bible, a text which is often granted a normative role in ethical decision-making.

On the other hand, scholars of the Hebrew Bible seem to have had very little difficulty in 'perceiving differences' between biblical perspectives on sex and perspectives which, we are told, reigned supreme elsewhere in the ancient world. 'Canaanite fertility religion', over against which Yahwism is often supposed to have defined itself, has frequently been characterized as something close to an orgy, complete with cultic prostitutes and vaguely defined 'sexual abuses in the service of religion' (Albright 1968: 132; cf. Albright 1957: 281; Wolff 1974: 14). The details of this picture of the Canaanites and their religion have now been challenged from a number of different directions, although it is too early to say with certainty whether the problem has primarily been a caricature of non-biblical religions by the authors of the biblical texts, a caricature of non-biblical religions by biblical scholars, or some combination of the

---

3.   Against the popular notion of a 'Judeo-Christian tradition' of sexual ethics, Boyarin (1993) has suggested that matters pertaining to sex and the body may in fact constitute one of the areas in which Rabbinic Judaism differed most radically from Christianity and from certain forms of Hellenistic Judaism such as that represented by, for instance, Philo.

two (cf. Hillers 1985; Oden 1987: 131-53; Bird 1989; Day 1991; Lemche 1991; Frymer-Kensky 1992: 199-202; Yee 1992: 196-97). In any case, until very recently discussions of Canaanite religion have tended to forge a conceptual link between sexual activity and 'pagan' religion. This tendency has made it difficult to consider in detail the actual nature and range of biblical attitudes toward sexual matters. Now that historians of ancient Israel seem less inclined to make absolute distinctions between 'Israelites' and 'Canaanites' (see, for example, Ahlström 1986; Coogan 1987), we may begin to find that descriptions of Canaanite religion increasingly adopt a more moderate and less orgiastic tone. It remains to be seen, however, whether the supposed link between sexual activity and non-Israelite religions will be abandoned on a more popular level.

All of the problems associated with these issues are compounded by the fact that biblical references to sexual activity are spread across several different genres of written discourse. The clearest statements about sexual practice in the Hebrew Bible are found in the collections of laws. The rhetoric is often formulated in terms of proscription and prescription: Israelites are forbidden to do this, and allowed to do that.[4] In some instances, Israel's identity as a chosen people seems to be tied in the legal texts to a certain sort of sexual practice (see, for example, Lev. 18.24-30). The abundance of this legal discourse on sexual and related matters frequently influences the ways in which other instances of sexual language or imagery in the Hebrew Bible are explained. Scholars often conceptualize biblical attitudes toward sexual activity in terms of forbidden and permitted behavior and, on occasion, treat narratives in which sexual scenes occur as if the stories must be explained in relation to the legal formulations.[5] Readers interpret the sexual actions of biblical characters primarily by comparing these actions to biblical laws and thereby pay insufficient attention to alternative modes of interpretation.[6]

4.   Proscriptions with regard to sexual practice are much more abundant in these laws than prescriptions, a fact which is important for evaluating the subsequent *effects* of biblical texts upon readers' attitudes toward sexual matters. Readers are encouraged to think about sex more in terms of what is forbidden than what is allowed.

5.   See, for instance, McCarter's discussion of Tamar's statement in 2 Sam. 13 that David will allow her half-brother to marry her (1984: 323-24). While McCarter does acknowledge various interpretations, his conclusion that 'the sacrilege in the present passage is incest' is based not on the text, where Tamar's words show no concern about incest, but rather on a comparison with the prohibitions against incest found in the biblical legal material.

6.   For a twist on the usual procedure of explaining narratives by appealing to

Yet biblical scholarship suggested long ago that the laws may have only a limited relevance, when they are relevant at all, for the interpretation of a particular biblical narrative (so, most famously, Wellhausen 1957). An analysis of the legal texts that touch upon sexual activity is insufficient (though obviously important) for a reconstruction of the biblical views of sexual matters. Some narratives clearly cohere with relevant legal texts, but our understanding of other narrative texts may be hindered by the assumption that the social presuppositions and concerns of legal formulations and narrative traditions are identical.

Moreover, although it is important to know that a particular act is forbidden or permitted by the religious authorities of a culture, the *meaning* of sex cannot be reduced to the specific proscriptions and prescriptions which build up around it. It is not enough to know that a particular act is forbidden. One must also ask to whom it is forbidden, and by whom, and why, and under what circumstances, and with what exceptions, and with what range of symbolic associations triggered by its commission. As these questions indicate, a great number of variables can determine the meaning of a sexual act in any particular context.

Of course, it is one thing to acknowledge the multiple meanings which sexual practice can trigger. It is quite another thing to suggest, in reference to any particular text, a plausible interpretation of the sexual events that take place there. We have relatively little evidence about the range of attitudes that might have been held in ancient Israel with regard to sexual matters. Moreover, narrative references to sexual activity seldom if ever seem to be made because of an interest in sexual matters per se, but arise instead in connection with other matters (cf. Barr 1992: 67; Biale 1992: 13). Consequently, these narratives usually contain little if any descriptive detail or overt evaluative discourse about sex.

In spite of the difficulties involved, a number of biblical scholars have made observations about the meaning and significance of sexual acts in the narratives of the Deuteronomistic History. An overview of some of the arguments that have been made about these biblical narrative sex acts, and of the relative strengths and weaknesses of these arguments, is a useful way to begin to situate the present study. The interdisciplinary perspective taken here may be able to shed light on aspects of the topic

laws, see Carmichael 1985. Carmichael argues that the legal traditions, and especially those in Deuteronomy, were created as a way of explaining older narrative traditions. The narratives with which Carmichael associates the laws on sexual practice are not those of the Deuteronomistic History analyzed here but rather those of the Pentateuch.

of sexual activity and biblical narrative to which these previous discussions have given insufficient attention. As Claudia Camp suggests, in some cases interpretations of biblical texts need to be challenged not because they utilize a 'bad' method, and not because they constitute a 'bad' use of an otherwise plausible method, but rather because their use of a single method has produced an interpretation which is too limited to be satisfactory (Camp 1985: 11; cf. Bal 1988a).

There are actually very few academic studies which have focused in detail on sexual activity and the biblical texts. If one is interested in considering the narrative literature in particular rather than the Hebrew Bible in general, there are fewer studies still. Most of the arguments that scholars have made about sex and the biblical narratives can be found in studies which are devoted to other issues. Primarily those studies which relate directly to the texts from the Deuteronomistic History analyzed in Chapter 4 are considered here. Other specific insights that have been made by biblical scholars are referred to in the textual discussions themselves, while the work of anthropologists studying sex and gender is considered in more detail in the next chapter.

Sex and the Deuteronomistic History: Previous Arguments

In an article published in 1966, Joseph Blenkinsopp attempted to examine the relationship between those sections of the Pentateuch attributed to the Yahwist and the so-called 'Succession History' which, in his opinion, begins in 2 Samuel 11. Blenkinsopp's analysis, which focuses upon what he considers to be thematic similarities between the two narratives, suggests that the Succession Narrative contains the theme of 'sin externalized in a sexual form which leads to death' (Blenkinsopp 1966: 48). According to Blenkinsopp, the theme manifests itself at least four times in the course of the document in relation to four women or groups of women: Bathsheba, Tamar, David's concubines, and Abishag. Restating this theme as 'the motif of the Woman who brings Death' (p. 52), Blenkinsopp argues that the theme can also be found in other ancient non-biblical texts, in the biblical book of Proverbs, and especially in the Yahwistic corpus.

Blenkinsopp devotes most of his discussion of the manifestation of this theme in the Succession Narrative to the story of David's sexual relation with Bathsheba. He suggests that 'there are some indications that she [Bathsheba] was not as blameless as a first reading of the text might suggest'. Blenkinsopp goes on to state that, far from being a minor point, the possibility that Bathsheba shared responsibility for the events of 2 Samuel 11 'would strengthen the pattern according to which death comes through the wiles of a woman' (p. 52); Bathsheba's shared responsibility would strengthen his argument that the motif of 'the Woman who brings Death' is a feature of the Succession History.

I argue in Chapter 4 that 'the wiles of a woman' actually play little if any role in the specific narratives from the Succession History which Blenkinsopp discusses. Nevertheless, Blenkinsopp does succeed in drawing attention to the role of sexual elements in the Deuteronomistic History, or at least in texts from that section of the History designated variously by biblical scholars as the 'Succession Narrative', the 'Succession History', or the 'Court History'. Blenkinsopp employs notions about sexual matters just as other scholars utilize perspectives on political or religious matters to analyze different segments of biblical literature.

In 1978, David Gunn published a study of the 'story of King David' which also takes into account the role played in that story by scenes involving sexual contact. Gunn's monograph is in a number of ways a groundbreaking work that challenges many conventional assumptions about both the 'Succession Narrative' (a term whose value Gunn himself disputes) and the methodologies used to examine it. The monograph has since become one of the most influential early attempts at a 'literary' approach to the Hebrew Bible. Gunn's discussion accepts and even expands upon Blenkinsopp's thematic category, 'the Woman who brings Death' (Gunn 1978: 43). Gunn considers the theme to be one of several indications that the story of David was based in part upon traditional folk motifs.

This application of the phrase 'the Woman who brings Death' to the female characters in the Succession Narrative is problematic, however. It is not entirely correct to imply that such female characters as Bathsheba, Tamar, the concubines of David or Abishag cause the deaths of the men with whom they are associated. Such an implication seems to be entailed when one makes the woman the subject of the 'bringing of death'. Yet in each of the instances from the Succession Narrative which Blenkinsopp and Gunn cite, the death of a male character is, as we shall see in more detail in Chapter 4, accomplished by other male characters. The women who appear in these stories are, as John Van Seters puts it, 'portrayed as completely *passive* as far as the death of the victim is concerned' (Van Seters 1987: 122, emphasis in original; cf. Exum 1993: 193). Van Seters notes as well that the women in the Succession Narrative (or, as he prefers, the Court History) do not actively solicit the sexual relationship, either: '[T]he woman is passive, resists the male's advances, or her role is unspecified'.[7] Van Seters therefore raises the possibility, which will be considered further in the present study, that the women in the Succession Narrative are neither subjects of murder nor subjects of sexual seduction.

It may be that, in choosing the thematic category 'the Woman who brings Death' as a tool for analysis, Blenkinsopp has fallen victim to a trap which is to a certain extent inherent in all thematic readings. As Mieke Bal has noted, thematic analyses have a tendency to subordinate form and structure to content, and to group disparate elements under a single rubric which is usually chosen in advance (Bal 1988a: 97-100). While it may not be possible or even desirable to avoid a consideration of 'themes' altogether, the risks involved need to be kept in mind. A recognition of these risks motivates in part the decision to include a narratological analysis of the texts analyzed in Chapter 4. A more detailed study of the actual structures of the texts themselves leads to a different formulation of the similarities between the texts than that of the theme of 'the Woman who brings Death'.

Blenkinsopp, in particular, tends to collocate a large number of otherwise heterogeneous texts under this category, playing down the differences between them in order to highlight a thematic similarity which he does not really defend with a close textual analysis. When Gunn, on the other hand, turns from a discussion of the genre of the Succession Narrative to a detailed literary interpretation of the stories contained therein, explicit references to the thematic category 'the Woman who brings Death' disappear. Once Gunn begins to deal with the actual details of the text, in other words, Blenkinsopp's formulation turns out to be of little help.

The one point on which Blenkinsopp, Gunn, and Van Seters all agree, however, is that sexual relations constitute a significant structuring principle in the Succession Narrative. Gunn articulates his own interpretation of that narrative corpus in terms of 'two major themes': 'David as king' in the 'political sphere', and 'David as man' in the 'private sphere'

---

7.   Van Seters goes on to make some very interesting, if brief, comparisons between the Hebrew Bible and selected Greek literary traditions with regard to the representation of women, 'love', and death. He associates the Court History on the basis of this ideology of sex and gender with the Homeric epics, and contrasts it with Greek tragedy and with certain ancient Near Eastern texts.

(Gunn 1978: 89). Gunn points out, and correctly so, that these two spheres are not entirely distinct in the story of David. Rather, the story develops in part through their interpenetration. Thus, the field of sexual relations cannot be confined exclusively to one of these two categories, the 'personal' or the 'political'. As Gunn argues, and as we will see in Chapter 4 below, the narratives develop in such a way that the boundaries between these two spheres are blurred significantly.

Perhaps Gunn's justly influential reading would have been even better had he avoided this opposition between 'personal' and 'political' altogether. Such oppositions, when deployed with reference to sexual matters, may be more helpful in illuminating modern Western literature than in interpreting stories from the Hebrew Bible. The biblical narratives bear few if any traces of interest in such an opposition so far as the representation of sexual activity is concerned. Interpreting sexual scenes at least in part as representations of the personality weaknesses and psychological conflicts of individual characters, Gunn comes close to adopting a perspective which has recently been criticized as an analytical starting point by such social historians as Robert Padgug. Padgug criticizes a perspective in which 'the sexual sphere is seen as the realm of psychology, while the public sphere is seen as the realm of politics and economics', and in which sexuality is conceptualized as something that occasionally 'slips over…into other spheres as well, spheres which would otherwise be definitely desexualized' (Padgug 1989: 17). The relationship between sexual matters and political matters in the biblical texts may be far more complicated than the opposition between the 'personal' and the 'political' can express. Indeed, in a more recent literary analysis which Gunn co-authored with Danna Nolan Fewell, an analysis which covers some of the same material as Gunn's earlier book (Fewell and Gunn 1993), much less use is made of this structuring principle.

Regina Schwartz has raised similar questions about the relevance of an opposition between a 'personal sphere' and a 'political sphere' for an understanding of biblical representations of sexuality. Schwartz focuses on questions of history, historiography, and identity: what kind of history does the biblical text constitute, and how does our answer to that question affect our understanding of Israel's self-conception? Exploring these matters, Schwartz emphasizes the role which sexual concerns play in Israel's narrative construction of its identity (see also Biale 1992: 11-32). Schwartz draws attention in particular to the interrelations between sex and power in the story of David.[8] She argues that in this story 'politics and sexuality are so deeply integrated as to be one, and it is anachronistic to even understand them as two different spheres of life' (Schwartz 1991: 46).

Schwartz implies that the instances of sexual contact in the stories about David are not easily accounted for by most scholarly discussions of the Deuteronomistic corpus. This implication seems to be generally accurate. Even so recent and compelling an account of the Deuteronomistic History as that presented by Theodore Mullen, for example, who wishes to 'address the present text of the deuteronomistic history as it might have functioned with respect to the community' struggling with the devastating reality of exile (Mullen 1993: 5), has scarcely anything to say about several prominent occurrences of sexual matters in 'the present text of the deuteronomistic history'. Mullen analyzes the story of David and Bathsheba primarily in relation to the role of Nathan and the appearance of Solomon, and he ignores the story of Amnon, Tamar, and Absalom altogether. When one considers Mullen's treatment of these two particular incidents in relation to the relative amount of textual space devoted to them in 'the present text of the deuteronomistic history', one sees the sagacity of Schwartz's suspicion that modern scholarly views of what might be important for inclusion in a historiographic text often obscure the actual focus and concerns of the texts themselves.

As an alternative way of conceptualizing the relationships between political and sexual matters in these narratives, an alternative which avoids the opposition between the 'personal' and the 'political', Schwartz points to the work of the structuralist anthropologist Claude Lévi-Strauss. In particular, she notes how Lévi-Strauss's kinship theories are based on the insight that men sometimes establish and negotiate their relations with one another through their exchange of women. Although Schwartz does not discuss Lévi-Strauss in detail, her appeal to this element of his work as an interpretive tool for reading the Hebrew Bible is a significant advance. I argue in the next chapter that Lévi-Strauss's theory about the exchange of women, as mediated and modified by the work of the anthropologist Gayle Rubin, provides a helpful lens for analyzing certain components of the representation of sexual relationships in biblical narrative.[9]

8.   These interrelations are also stressed by Fewell and Gunn (1993).

9.   Schwartz does not specifically cite Rubin's analysis. However, Schwartz's use of the phrase 'traffic in women' (1991: 52) is apparently an allusion to Rubin's influential article, which carries that title (1975).

Indeed, Rubin's discussion of the exchange of women and of the social relations that result from this exchange sheds light on other stories as well, stories in which sexual activity is not always explicit but in which David's power is consolidated in part through his ability to take women from other men, whether fathers or husbands. This feature of David's story has often been noted and has been interpreted from literary perspectives (for example, Linafelt 1992) and from historical-critical perspectives (for example, Levenson and Halpern 1980). Scholars other than Schwartz have not analyzed this aspect of the story of David in relation to anthropological theory, however, although the relevant anthropological literature has not been entirely ignored by scholars of ancient Israelite and Near Eastern literature and history.[10] It is sufficient to note here that, by making explicit the need to consider a broader system of cultural dynamics and gender differentials when interpreting the sexual acts in biblical narratives, Schwartz opens a door onto the problematic which the present project explores in more detail.

The fact that the biblical instances of sexual contact occur in texts which assume a distant cultural context is also recognized, though from a somewhat different perspective, by Tikva Frymer-Kensky (1992). Frymer-Kensky's study attempts to evaluate the significance of the shift in Israel from a polytheistic culture that included both gods and goddesses to a monotheism in which goddesses were eliminated from orthodox Yahwism. This attempt takes her from a consideration of the nature and functions of ancient Near Eastern goddesses to an examination of, among other things, the attitudes toward gender and sexuality that one finds in the Hebrew Bible. In carrying out her examination, Frymer-Kensky deploys many of the traditional tools of the historian of the ancient Near East (including philology, historical criticism, and so forth). The result is an excellent contribution to the study of ancient Israel and its historical context which sheds a great deal of light upon biblical ideas about gender and sex.[11]

10. Liverani, for example, includes a discussion of the exchange of women in an analysis of certain economic aspects of the Amarna letters (1979: 31-33). His study is explicitly indebted to Mauss's anthropological theory of gift exchange (see Mauss 1990) which lies behind the analyses of Lévi-Strauss and Rubin discussed in the next chapter. Already in 1938 Burrows suggested the relevance of Mauss's work for an understanding of Israelite marriage (see, for example, Burrows 1938: 11).

11. For a study of sexual imagery in Mesopotamian literature that is in many ways complementary to Frymer-Kensky's work, see Leick 1994.

Frymer-Kensky's discussion does not claim to be a complete analysis of the narrative literature which refers to sexual contact, but she does refer to that literature (including the Deuteronomistic History) in the course of her argument. One of the places where she considers biblical narratives that include instances of sexual contact is in her discussion of biblical gender imagery. Frymer-Kensky suggests there that female characters in the Hebrew Bible do not use sexual attraction as a tool 'to seduce and then deceive men' (Frymer-Kensky 1992: 140). Instead, they seek out sexual activity either for procreation (for example, in Genesis, Tamar, Rachel and Leah) or for pleasure (for example, Potiphar's wife); or, like Bathsheba and Tamar in 2 Samuel, they do not seek it out at all but rather have it forced upon them. Frymer-Kensky thus emphasizes a point also made by Van Seters: although stories that are structured around the active sexual seduction of men by women certainly exist, the biblical narrative texts do not include many examples of such stories.[12]

Frymer-Kensky links this argument to another thesis which is more questionable. She suggests that there is in biblical thought an 'essential similarity between male and female', a 'gender-free concept of humanity' which refused to associate some qualities with men and others with women (Frymer-Kensky 1992: 141-43). For Frymer-Kensky, this 'essential similarity' is a corollary of monotheism, since a pantheon of gods and goddesses (whose interactions could in some manner model relations between men and women) has now been replaced by a single deity. Frymer-Kensky does contrast this biblical perspective on gender with the actual living conditions and social structures of ancient Israel. Indeed, she recognizes explicitly that the biblical texts themselves reveal a social structure in which the social inequality of men and women was assumed. Nevertheless, she insists upon the 'essential sameness of the sexes' in biblical thought, which was in her opinion only modified under the influence of Greek thought during the Hellenistic period.[13]

12. I am less certain than Frymer-Kensky that Genesis does not utilize aspects, at least, of this theme. The case of Potiphar's wife in particular (Gen. 39.6-20) does seem to be constructed around a certain male fear of *active* female sexuality. However, Frymer-Kensky's point has considerable merit with regard to the Deuteronomistic History.

13. Frymer-Kensky refers to a number of negative attitudes toward women that appear in postbiblical Judaism as 'gifts of the Greeks' (1992: 203-12). Her argument attributes a perceived degeneration of Israelite thought to its contact with Hellenistic culture and, in the process, draws a sharp contrast between 'biblical' and 'Greek' thought which may oversimplify. For an influential discussion and critique of certain

Frymer-Kensky's conclusion that there exists an 'essential similarity between male and female in biblical thought' (p. 141) is based primarily on her argument that female characters do not deploy 'feminine' means of achieving their goals. For example, they seldom use their beauty or sexual wiles to obtain what they want from male characters. Nevertheless, Frymer-Kensky's own discussion makes clear that such biblical texts as the laws pertaining to female sexuality simply assume the 'inferior social position of women' (pp. 119-20). The basic *social inequality* between men and women which Frymer-Kensky herself emphasizes when analyzing legal texts may be so pervasive in the Hebrew Bible precisely because a *fundamental difference* between men and women is assumed by those who wrote the texts. If such differences are not spelled out in detail, it may well be the case that, far from being nonexistent, they were simply taken for granted.[14]

Frymer-Kensky's discussion, which includes many valuable insights and which covers issues far beyond the scope of the present project, underscores the fact that the analysis of biblical views on sexual activity cannot be carried out in isolation from an analysis of biblical views on gender. The two elements are, as she recognizes, related in significant but complicated ways. Indeed, this crucial point also emerges quite clearly in the anthropological studies of gender and of sex discussed in the next chapter.

It is therefore no surprise that many feminist analyses of biblical

uses of the opposition between 'Greek' and 'Hebrew' thought, see Barr 1961; 1966. It is interesting to note the continued but variable appeal of this binary framework in discussions of biblical notions of sex, gender, and the body. Now that it has become somewhat more acceptable to criticize traditional attitudes toward sex and the body, the 'anti-sex' or 'anti-body' attitude is sometimes seen as a relic of 'Greek' influence upon the Jewish tradition which, it is claimed, had a more positive attitude toward such matters. When one compares this sort of interpretation to, for example, older contrasts between Israelite religion and the supposed 'orgiastic' religion of the Canaanites (which Frymer-Kensky rightly criticizes), one realizes how easily carica-tures of 'paganism' continue to serve as a foil for those elements of Judaism and Christianity which one wishes to emphasize and rehabilitate for a later age. Thus, the very real historical and literary questions at stake in these discussions need to be approached with a great deal of care to note the many different strands within and overlaps among 'Judaism', 'Christianity', and 'Hellenism'.

14. This is not to imply, of course, that an assumed fundamental difference between male and female must always take the same form. Laqueur (1990) points out that some ancient accounts of such differences understand 'male' and 'female' less as polar opposites than as superior and inferior versions of one another.

literature consider the sexual aspects of the Deuteronomistic History in terms of the assumptions about gender which underlie them. A number of these analyses (for instance, Trible 1984: 37-91; Exum 1993: 170-201; Fewell and Gunn 1993: 132-36, 142-45; Bal 1988b; Keefe 1993) focus on texts (such as Judg. 19 and 2 Sam. 13) that depict scenes of rape or sexual violence. One issue which has consequently been highlighted is the relation between gender and power. Attention is increasingly given to the fact that power seems to be unevenly distributed among the characters in these stories, and that the female characters are usually represented as having less power than the male characters.

Relating the question of sexual activity to issues of gender and power suggests that it is crucial to consider the connotations of individual texts in terms of wider networks of cultural associations and symbolic meanings. 'Sex' cannot be abstracted from other elements of the cultural matrix from which the biblical texts emerged; it must instead be seen in terms of its connections to other aspects of the social world as well as to meanings presupposed by those texts. Precisely because readers of biblical narratives need to take larger cultural frameworks into account when interpreting sexual scenes, the advantages of anthropology as an interpretive tool ought to be weighed carefully.

This fact was already noted in a frequently cited study of sexual practice and the Hebrew Bible which was published in 1959: Raphael Patai's *Sex and Family in the Bible and the Middle East.* Although Patai addressed the Hebrew Bible as a whole rather than the Deuteronomistic History in particular, his utilization of anthropological literature justifies a brief consideration of his work here. Patai's monograph, as its title indicates, attempts to take a comparative approach to biblical views of sex and family. It considers sexual activity especially in relation to marriage and family structures.[15] Patai recognizes that biblical references to these subjects are often characterized by 'brevity' and an 'allusive style which takes for granted knowledge of context and background not possessed

15. Kinship structures also form the primary context for an understanding of sexual relations in the overview by Richter (1978). Unlike Patai and the present work, however, Richter interprets these phenomena by way of a somewhat traditional historical-critical approach to Israel's history and religion and so gives little attention to the contributions of anthropological literature for reconstructing the symbolic values attributed to sex and gender by the biblical texts. The recent work by Eilberg-Schwartz (1990), on the other hand, does rely extensively on anthropological material, but primarily in relation to the legal texts.

as a rule by the twentieth-century Westerner' (Patai 1959: 14). Thus, he suggests that one must look beyond the bounds of the narrative in order to understand the context of assumptions within which the texts were meaningful for an ancient audience.

While Patai acknowledges the relevance of ancient Near Eastern literary and archaeological evidence for reconstructing the cultural context of the Hebrew Bible, he suggests that this knowledge can be supplemented with information about what he calls the 'folk life of the Middle East' (p. 15). In other words, Patai is willing to explore the possibility that ethnographic information might shed light upon the Hebrew Bible—not the only light, to be sure, but a potentially illuminating one nonetheless. Unfortunately, the ethnographic information upon which Patai relies is now substantially outdated. Moreover, his choice of ethnographic materials is determined by assumptions about the Hebrew Bible which are much less widely shared today than they were at the time when Patai wrote his monograph.[16] In addition, Patai has a fairly simplistic notion of the extent to which one can move from the biblical texts to an anterior social world.

Despite these flaws, Patai's attempt is valuable inasmuch as he gives his reader a sense of the range of evidence which is potentially relevant to the topic of sexual ideology. Many of the questions he raises are still relevant, even if his answers are no longer plausible. The suggestion that anthropological literature can assist the interpreter in understanding biblical perspectives on sexual practice will be considered in more detail in the next chapter, though much more attention will be given to methodological developments that have taken place since the publication of Patai's book.

All of these projects contribute to an understanding of the role of sexual activity within the Deuteronomistic History. Nevertheless, previous approaches to the question focus primarily on either narrative structure or historical and social context. Little attention is given to the influence of cultural assumptions about sexual matters on the structure of the texts.

---

16. For example, Patai assumes that the earliest Israelites were pastoral nomads and that the nomadic lifestyle continued to influence the beliefs and practices of the Israelites. He thus bases his analyses primarily upon accounts of the (so-called) pastoral nomads of the nineteenth and early- to mid-twentieth centuries. Many of his assumptions about pastoral nomadism have now been called into question (cf. Gottwald 1979; Lemche 1985).

Historical studies are usually sensitive to the gap between our world and the world presupposed by the biblical text (although this sensitivity may sometimes be less apparent in matters of sex and gender than in other areas). Yet studies of that historical gap, though they generally appeal to the texts as evidence, sometimes pay insufficient attention to the actual literary dynamics of the texts being utilized. More recent literary approaches frequently criticize historical methods on precisely this point. Literary critics attempt to remedy the failure of biblical scholars to take into account the nature of narrative discourse, and, in the process, they are able to highlight many features that have been ignored in the quest for historical 'facts'. On the other hand, some literary readings show little interest in the narratives' social and cultural matrix. Literary critics uninterested in such matters can scarcely be criticized for not producing something which they had no interest in producing. Nevertheless, it has been insufficiently noted that the very structures of the texts are in part the result of a social or symbolic world which these texts presuppose.

Outside of biblical scholarship, however, there has been an explosion of interest in recent years in the variable meanings that people have attributed to sexual practice and in the variability of the practices themselves. The projects which have focused in one way or another upon sexual matters appear in fields as diverse as anthropology, sociology, literary criticism, history, and philosophy. In the field of classical studies alone, for example, there is a veritable sub-discipline devoted to the exploration of such topics (see, for example, Dover 1989 [1978]; Keuls 1985; Halperin 1990; Winkler 1990; Halperin, Winkler, and Zeitlin [eds.] 1989; Cantarella 1992; Veyne 1985; Rousselle 1988; Richlin 1993) and similar investigations have begun to appear which focus upon the conceptualization of sexual matters in the histories of Judaism (for example, Boyarin 1993; Eilberg-Schwartz [ed.] 1990; 1992; 1994; Biale 1992) and Christianity (for example, Brooten 1985; Brown 1988; Boswell 1980; cf. Rousselle 1988).

This research has generally emphasized the value of contextualizing sexual matters and the representation of such matters in literary discourse. While sexual activity and the meanings associated with it were once considered to be relatively stable and unchanging, it has become increasingly apparent that sexual practices, 'sexual meanings' (Ortner and Whitehead 1981), and perhaps even the subjectivities of the individuals behind such practices and meanings are actually quite fluid and variable. If it was once thought that sexual practice, sexual identity, gender identity, and sexual desire were matters primarily for the fields of psychology and biology, this assumption has come under sharp attack by those who argue that society, culture, and history are the primary matrices for the production of human subjects as sexual subjects (cf., for example, Padgug 1989; Foucault 1978; 1985; 1986; Rubin 1975; 1984; Weeks 1985).

While attempts to contextualize the biblical narratives generally rely upon established historical-critical methods, the present study will follow a path suggested by Patai and others. Like Patai, I assume that anthropological research may shed light upon the cultural and symbolic context of certain biblical texts. However, in the pages that follow I will not only attempt to account for anthropological research that has been carried out since the publication of Patai's work. I will also argue that an interpretation of biblical literature which makes use of anthropological materials needs to explicate its understanding of the relationship between that interpretation and the methods of contemporary literary criticism. The narratives that deal with sexual activity will be interpreted more adequately when both anthropological and literary questions are taken into consideration.

Chapter 2

AN ANTHROPOLOGICAL FRAMEWORK FOR READING

Introduction

The present chapter and that which follows will stress the value of an interdisciplinary approach to the study of the representation of sexual practice in biblical narratives. The position adopted here recognizes that links exist between literature and its social and cultural context. Such a position can itself be seen as a product of an academic environment in which fruitful interaction among various disciplines has become increasingly accepted. One sees today a certain willingness to transgress traditional disciplinary boundaries in the pursuit of new questions and new objects of study. Thus, one well-known commentator speaks of the 'blurred genres' of contemporary academic discourse (Geertz 1983: 19-35). In particular, such fields as literary studies, cultural anthropology, and history are increasingly developing not in isolation from one another, but rather in a productive interdisciplinary conversation (cf., for example, Veeser [ed.] 1989; Hunt [ed.] 1989; White 1973; 1978; 1987; Clifford and Marcus [eds.] 1986; Clifford 1988; Geertz 1988).

Within the field of Hebrew Bible studies, discussions about interdisciplinary analysis most often focus on the relationship between newer approaches and the more established methods of historical criticism. The general acceptance of the historical-critical methods of biblical interpretation has frequently led proponents of alternative approaches to define themselves over against these methods (see for example Polzin 1989: 1-17). This means of approaching interdisciplinary analysis, though easily understood, has had some unfortunate consequences. For example, it occasionally leads to a caricature of 'historical criticism', which is made to appear much more monolithic an enterprise than, in fact, it probably ever has been. Moreover, a defining of the issues in a particular manner (such as 'historical criticism *versus* newer approaches') can prevent an exploration of the possible relations *between* various newer approaches.

This situation may be changing. There is a growing number of scholars who are interested in the relationships between careful literary analyses of the biblical texts, on the one hand, and analyses which make use of insights from the social sciences, on the other hand (see, for example, Gottwald 1985; Jobling 1990; 1991a; Mullen 1993; Segovia 1995). Such an interest underlies this project as well.

The present chapter considers some of the ways in which cultural anthropology can aid in the reading of biblical narrative. This discussion is followed by an overview of specific emphases from contemporary anthropological debates about sex, gender, honor and power that shed light upon the specific biblical narratives which are analyzed in Chapter 4. Chapter 3 will then address literary analysis in more detail. A narrato-logical method of textual analysis is discussed as is the integration of the results of such an approach with an anthropological perspective. That discussion will return us to the issue taken up here: the nature of an 'anthropological reading'.

On the Nature and Importance of Anthropological Reading

There is a long history of relations between the study of the Hebrew Bible and ancient Israel, on the one hand, and the disciplines of anthropology and sociology, on the other hand (see Rogerson 1984; 1989; McNutt 1990: 24-35; Leach 1982). In recent years, however, insights and theories derived from these disciplines have impacted scholarship on the history and literature of ancient Israel to a greater extent than had previously been the case. There is now an extensive body of literature on the social, cultural, and material history of ancient Israel which self-con-sciously utilizes models from the social sciences. Even a cursory exami-nation of the various projects listed under such rubrics as 'sociological approaches to the Old Testament' (Wilson 1984) or 'anthropological approaches to the Old Testament' (Lang [ed.] 1985) reveals that such studies are by no means uniform in methodology. On the contrary, they represent a quite heterogeneous set of approaches applied to a wide range of texts and historical periods.[1]

1.   Important studies include Gottwald 1979; 1985; Wilson 1977; 1980; Hopkins 1985; Lemche 1985; Meyers 1988; Flanagan 1988; McNutt 1990; Eilberg-Schwartz 1990; Matthews and Benjamin (eds.) 1993; Steinberg 1993; Mullen 1993; Simkins 1994; Coote and Whitelam 1987. For an examination of biblical texts by an anthro-pologist which is in many ways distinct from later anthropological approaches to biblical literature and history, see Leach 1969.

The present study differs from some of the previous 'anthropological approaches' to the Hebrew Bible in that it focuses less upon the history and social structures of ancient Israel, as these are generally understood, and more upon a specific group of texts. The interest in anthropological and sociological models in the field of biblical studies has been evident primarily among scholars who identify themselves as historians but who have come to suspect the methodological validity of traditional assumptions about the use of biblical materials in the reconstruction of Israelite history. As J.W. Rogerson puts it, '[W]hat Old Testament scholars have wanted, rightly or wrongly, from anthropology, is help with understanding aspects of Israel's history' (Rogerson 1989: 19; cf. Lemche 1988: 68-9). A key element of this turn to social-scientific models among some historians of ancient Israel has been the recognition that the biblical narratives may not constitute a reliable source for the reconstruction of Israel's past, since they often seem to be, to use Barr's terms, 'story' rather than 'history' (Barr 1980: 1-17), and moreover a story that was probably written long after the time period which it claims to recount. Consequently, anthropological and sociological models are sometimes deployed *in explicit contrast to* the biblical texts, precisely because it is the history of Israel rather than the meaning of particular biblical texts which has been designated as the object of study. This situation may help to account for the fact that symbolic anthropology, which emphasizes the interpretation of meaning, has had a much less significant impact in the field of Hebrew Bible studies than have approaches which focus on social organization or on the interrelations between social structures and ecological or material history.

The present study emphasizes symbolic and ideological questions; questions about the social organization or material history of Israel are less prominent. Attention is given to certain cultural assumptions about sexual activity and gender which seem to have influenced the shape of the biblical text. Stated another way, this study primarily addresses the 'domain of notions' rather than the 'domain of actions' (for an application of this distinction, see Flanagan 1988; cf. Fewell and Gunn 1993: 13). The predominant focus will be upon ideas, meanings, and mentalities, partially encoded in and partially presupposed by the biblical texts. Indeed, since the meanings of particular texts will constitute its primary object, this study might be described more appropriately as a literary interpretation than as an instance of social history. Nevertheless, it is the sort of literary interpretation which seeks to explore the complex interrelations between literary discourse and what has been called 'implicit social knowledge' (Lancaster 1992: xv).

A helpful way of entering this complicated set of issues is by considering the manner in which social and cultural assumptions necessarily enter into the process of *reading* ancient texts (cf. Wilson 1984: 3-6; Malina 1991a; 1991b). One of the most significant developments in literary and semiotic theory over the past two decades is the increased attention given to the role of reading and reading conventions in the production of textual meaning (see, for example, Suleiman and Crosman [eds.] 1980; Tompkins [ed.] 1980; Culler 1975; 1981; 1982). The meaning of a literary text is no longer considered to reside exclusively in 'the text itself'; rather, meaning is generated by the interaction of a reading subject, textual structures, and reading conventions, and this interaction takes place within a social context. This theoretical observation has points of similarity and overlap with hermeneutical discussions more familiar to biblical scholars, for hermeneutic theorists also argue that textual meaning depends in part upon the tradition and horizon of expectations in which the interpreter of texts is unavoidably embedded (see, for example, Gadamer 1985; Ricoeur 1981). For the purposes of the present discussion, a reader's presuppositions always include, in particular, presuppositions about the nature of social life and about the significance of particular social relations and cultural processes.

Assumptions about social structures as well as cultural, symbolic meanings probably influence most readings of biblical narratives. Yet the ways in which these assumptions impact the reading process can be quite complicated, and they depend in part upon the variable amount of cultural information contained within any particular text. Thus, the texts to be examined in Chapter 4 are composed of various elements of narrative discourse: action sequences, dialogues, narratorial comment, and so forth. In order to interpret the texts, readers make sense of these elements and of the interrelations among them. However, this process often seems to require a large amount of information about cultural assumptions *presupposed by* the text, information that is not spelled out for us explicitly *in* the text. A great deal is necessarily concluded by the reader on the basis of inference and supposition.

For example, characters within the biblical narrative frequently act *in response to* the actions and words of other characters. Yet the motivations for these responses, and the logic that would explain why a character reacts in a particular way, are often not specified. Readers may consequently be uncertain about the precise manner in which, within an ancient context, the reacting character might have been understood to interpret the actions of the character to which he or she responds. This uncertainty exists even though it is obvious that some sort of interpretation of one character's actions by another character must be posited in order to make sense of the narrative.

To anticipate some specific cases discussed in more detail below: readers of Judges 19 generally assume that the Levite who appears there makes some sort of interpretation of the sexual advances made against him by the men of Gibeah, and that this interpretation motivates the actions which he takes toward his concubine. In 2 Samuel 16 Absalom seems to know that his own sexual activity will be interpreted by those who see that he has had intercourse with his father's concubines. Thus, the narrative sexual actions function as semiotic acts *within* the represented story-world. They are messages of sorts, acts of communication addressed to other characters within the narrative—and, by extension, to readers of the narrative, ancient or modern. In neither of these two examples is a complete explanation given in the story about the meaning of the sexual acts that are recounted.[2] Yet a meaningful interpretation (or, possibly, a culturally determined range of interpretations) of the sexual contact by certain characters within the narrative is clearly presupposed by the narrative. The logic of the narrative seems to rely on the assumption that an audience will be able to infer this interpretation and judge the characters accordingly. Our own interpretation of these passages thus depends on our knowledge of some sort of fund of presupposed cultural beliefs in the light of which the narrated events make sense, but which is not supplied by the text. Without assuming premises of one sort or another about the range of meanings which might be attributed to sexual activity, we may find it impossible to articulate an interpretation of these stories.

Such situations arise quite frequently during the process of reading biblical narratives. At many points biblical literature is ambiguous, particularly to the modern reader who is removed temporally and culturally from the world in which the texts were written. Even when we take into account the polysemy of language and literature in general, some ambiguity results from the cultural gap that separates modern Western readers, scholarly or otherwise, from our object of analysis. We lack a

2.   We shall see in Chapter 4 that in the second case, the beginnings of an explanation are given by Ahithophel, one of the other characters.

knowledge of the social and cultural conventions, the semiotic and symbolic networks of meaning, which would have simply been assumed at the time in which these stories were written and which ancient authors, like all authors, counted on for the successful communication of their message (see Culler 1981: 18-43; cf. Weems 1992: 27). Lacking such knowledge, we fall necessarily upon our own traditions and 'common sense' to fill in the gaps of meaning which result.

Indeed, while the meaning of almost any text, ancient or modern, seems to entail the use of implicit cultural assumptions, the situation is more severe in the case of biblical literature than in the case of, say, a modern novel or historical narrative. In his recent examination of Israelite attitudes toward 'nature', Ronald Simkins attempts to account for this fact by suggesting that Israel was a 'high context society':

> In high context societies a rich common culture is assumed by all the members of the society, and the identity of individual members is defined in terms of that culture. Moreover, because the society is based upon a common culture, each individual requires an adequate understanding of that culture in order to function well within the society (Simkins 1994: 41).

As Simkins points out, a text which is produced in a 'high context society' where 'members of the society have been socialized into shared ways of perceiving and acting' tends to contain relatively little descriptive detail. In contrast, texts produced in a 'low context society', in which authors cannot so easily assume that their readers share a common culture and worldview, contain much more detail and explanation, and necessarily so (Simkins 1994: 41-42; cf. Malina 1991b: 19-20; Hall 1976: 91-101).

This opposition can surely be overstated.[3] All societies, including ancient Israel, contain groups and classes of people who can be differentiated from one another on the basis of their social assumptions. Indeed, literature can function precisely to erase or obscure points of conflict and disagreement between different groups within the same society. Nevertheless, if it is not applied in a rigid manner, the distinction

---

3.   One might take issue, for example, with the following statement: 'Low context societies like the United States...require little knowledge of culture in order for their members to get along, nor does culture play a determinative role in forming individual identity' (Simkins 1994: 41). I prefer to stress the relative and heuristic value of the contrast between high and low context societies; both necessarily rely upon a knowledge of shared cultural assumptions for successful communication and for the formation of identity, but to different degrees.

between high and low context societies may help to explain why the Hebrew narratives often *assume* rather than *explain* the cultural presuppositions of their authors and audiences. It may also account for some of the difficulties experienced by modern readers who are accustomed to reading texts with more descriptive explanation and who are socialized in a culture which does not share all of the cultural knowledge presupposed by the authors of the biblical texts.

Much of this cultural knowledge is lost to us entirely. It is doubtful that we will ever read and understand the biblical text exactly as ancient Israelites understood it, even if we grant the possibility of diverse interpretations among the Israelites themselves. Nevertheless, we can attempt to reconstruct approximations to such meanings, approximations which, as literary interpretations, can be judged more or less plausible in any given instance.

Anthropological information, when used cautiously as a heuristic aid for reading, can be a valuable tool for such an enterprise. As a result of the observation, analysis, and interpretation of various cultures carried out by anthropologists over the years, there is now a large body of scholarship devoted to exploring the sorts of conventional assumptions and 'implicit meanings' (Douglas 1975) which circulate or have circulated in a vast number of cultures and subcultures across time and space. This body of scholarship helps us to recognize some of the ways in which human societies construe the significance of certain social relationships and processes. Such recognition serves a heuristic function to the extent that we are able to formulate questions and hypotheses about the significance of social relationships and processes recounted in ancient texts. We cannot simply assume that the ancient Israelites construed the significance of social phenomena in the same ways as other cultures studied by anthropologists. However, we can ask about the extent to which the anthropological literature *does and does not* help us in making sense of the assumptions underlying the biblical texts.

It is important to acknowledge that we cannot expect a perfect 'fit' between such evidence as we have for the culture and ideas of ancient Israel, on the one hand, and the ideas of other cultures which have been uncovered and explicated by anthropologists, on the other. Indeed, it would be a most 'unanthropological' gesture to suggest that the culture and society of ancient Israel were *identical* to any other culture and society. It is precisely the recognition that each culture has its own particular characteristics, which are easily misunderstood by outside observers, that led to the important role assigned by cultural anthropology to fieldwork and participant observation.

Moreover, while the biblical text may serve as an 'informant' about the beliefs and assumptions held by ancient Israelites (so McNutt 1990: 36), the text is itself an imperfect source of ethnographic data. We cannot assume that the Bible offers a transparent window into the world of ancient Israel, even in those places where it appears on the surface to provide substantial amounts of information about Israelite culture. It is far more likely that the biblical text offers a series of glimpses of the sort of world which was deemed possible, or in some cases desirable, by those individuals and groups among whom the biblical texts originated. Some portions of this picture may constitute a fairly accurate portrait of life as it really took place in ancient Israel. Other portions may constitute a very filtered version of such life. Still other portions probably constitute little more than wishful thinking on the part of those responsible for producing the texts. The picture that we have is always presented from a particular perspective which influenced its shape and helped to determine both what was included and what was excluded from the literary record.

Emphasizing this point, Carol Meyers argues that the Hebrew Bible was written primarily from the perspective of an urban, male, literate, priestly elite writing about events from which they were temporally far removed; the result is that much of the Hebrew Bible contains mainly ideology rather than a historically accurate picture of Israelite behavior in the periods which it claims to represent (Meyers 1988: 11-13). Meyers's argument echoes other claims about the biblical texts made over the years (cf., for example, Smith 1987; Garbini 1988; Lemche 1988; Dever 1990; Davies 1992). Given such claims, we must be cautious about using the biblical texts to make statements about 'Israelite culture', let alone 'Israelite history'. The point here is not that the search for the historical Israel ought to be abandoned; rather, it is to recognize that the ways in which the biblical texts have been employed in such searches often fail to take sufficiently into account the nature of these texts as literary representations, written long after the periods they claim to describe. To use the terminology of Philip Davies, 'biblical Israel' (that is, the picture of Israel that we find in the Hebrew Bible) cannot simply be conflated with the actual historical society (or societies) which existed in Israel and Judah during the Iron Age (Davies 1992); and this fact is as important for the social or cultural historian as it is for the more traditional historian of great events or biographer of famous persons.

Such a conclusion does not force us to abandon the analysis of the biblical texts as instances of culturally determined and socially shaped discourse. Inasmuch as some sort of a picture is drawn in these texts, we are given evidence for the sorts of events and persons (and interrelations between them) which could be conceptualized, which could be considered possible, and which could be projected in a text that claimed to recount a people's past. As Mieke Bal has put it, the events that take place in biblical narrative, and the persons involved in those events, can be used as evidence for what was 'thinkable' in ancient Israel (Bal 1988b: 33); and it is precisely here, by analyzing and interpreting *that which can be thought*, that we can learn a great deal about the beliefs and ideological assumptions of those who told these stories, even if we are skeptical about our ability to reconstruct the actual historical existence of the persons or events that are recounted.

Anthropologists have produced a considerable amount of material on the relations among sex, gender, honor, and social status. It is part of my argument that some of this material is relevant for an understanding of biblical literature and of the use to which sexual activity is put in this literature. Anthropological discussions of the meanings attributed to sexual activity assist in the recognition of relations which human beings make between various phenomena associated with sexual activity. In a number of ways the anthropological discussions help us to raise important questions about the significance of sexual activity within the biblical narratives. At those points in the text where implicit, conventional meaning seems to be called for, anthropological studies often supply information about *possible* meanings of sexual activity which originate from other cultures. In some cases it will be possible to articulate an interpretation of the narrative in the light of the anthropological material, particularly if that material suggests an explanation for textual features that have previously remained opaque.

Anthropological concepts can help us to construct and continually reassess our reading frames—that is to say, our ideas about the possible context of symbols and beliefs in terms of which the texts seem to make sense—in a way that at least mitigates our tendency to interpret biblical texts in terms of our own assumptions.[4] Anthropological concepts, used

4.   On the notion of 'framing' as a means for explaining our attempts at contextualization in the process of interpretation, see Culler 1988: xiii-xiv; Bal and Bryson 1991: 175-80; Bryson 1992; Bal 1991b: 6-7.

judiciously, may help us tease out certain implicit premises of the texts that we are trying to read. The use of anthropology frequently causes us to distance ourselves from at least part of what passes as 'common sense' in our own culture. Thus, it can enable us to develop a reading practice which is concerned to acknowledge, rather than gloss over, the cultural differences between our society and that in which the biblical texts emerged.

The results of anthropological investigation are based, at least in theory, on the actions and words of real people. There are thus problems involved in applying such evidence to texts produced at other times and places. I do not claim that ancient Israelites always acted like the figures of ethnographic literature. Nor do literary characters always embody the conventions of the culture in which they emerge. Indeed, the effect of literature is often achieved by a transgression of cultural conventions. However, it is impossible for communication to occur without some idea of the implicit meanings which circulate in a culture, and the actions of literary characters are always interpreted against a background of cultural premises to which they are considered to respond in various ways. The question that remains is whether cultural premises postulated on the basis of anthropological evidence cohere with the textual elements. This question can only be answered after an attempt at anthropological interpretation has actually been carried out. An anthropological reading must finally be judged, at that point, in the same way that other readings are judged: on the basis of its plausibility in the light of information brought forward by the scholar for consideration by the wider scholarly community.

Before detailing the anthropological information which has influenced the readings to follow, three additional caveats about the process of anthropological reading must be made. First, as others have noted, any use of the results of another discipline requires a familiarity with the methods and assumptions of that discipline. It is essential, when attempting to make comparative arguments based upon elements of anthropological discussion, to understand the context in which those discussions were initially generated. Such an understanding may forestall hasty comparisons which could lead to implausible results.

In addition, the interpretive and constructive nature of the endeavor must always be remembered. While one can seek to persuade others of the relevance of certain anthropological information for biblical interpretation, the results of anthropological fieldwork or theorizing do not lead inevitably to the one true meaning of a biblical text; rather, they open up various possibilities. Indeed, faced with multiple scenarios brought forward by anthropologists, one could always argue, and justifiably so, that there is no one necessary conclusion to be reached about the interrelations among various cultural and social phenomena (cf. Lemche 1985). Thus, the present study is concerned not with scientific method as traditionally conceived but rather with heuristic comparisons and the evaluation of the plausibility of various interpretations.[5]

Moreover, it is to be expected that the results of a comparative analysis will not be entirely positive. Use of comparative material surely will reveal not only ways in which an anthropological frame coheres with a given text, but also ways in which it fails to do so. Such a failure can itself be a significant finding, inasmuch as the particular characteristics of the texts under consideration are thereby highlighted by way of contrast.

Elements of an Anthropological Frame

The following discussion focuses upon three areas of anthropological debate out of which we can generate heuristic questions and interpretive tools for approaching the texts considered in Chapter 4. These areas address the interrelations among sex, gender, and prestige structures; the interrelations between a competitive notion of masculinity and a concern about female chastity; and the role of the exchange of women in male relationships. These concepts, which have substantial overlap, will be presented by way of a dialogue with contemporary anthropological literature. This discussion is intended to be suggestive rather than exhaustive. I will articulate a somewhat general 'frame' for my readings. The primary concern is the reconstruction of possible cultural premises in terms of which plausible readings can be defended.

Sex, Gender, and the Structure of Prestige
Sherry Ortner and Harriet Whitehead emphasize the relation between sexual matters and the structure of prestige in an essay introducing an

---

5.   Tolbert points out that biblical scholars who use sociological or anthropological material sometimes 'emphasize the scientific nature of these methods'. She goes on to suggest that this emphasis is 'a way of avoiding the mounting critique of historical positivism in biblical studies' (1993: 268; cf. D.B. Martin 1993: 109-10). Yet as Tolbert points out, the critique of positivism is, if anything, even more developed in anthropology (see, for example, Clifford and Marcus [eds.] 1986; Clifford 1988; Rosaldo 1989; Fabian 1983).

important collection of studies on 'sexual meanings' (Ortner and Whitehead 1981). Ortner and Whitehead note that, while kinship and marriage have long been recognized as important social contexts for the meanings attributed to gender and sex, the role of prestige structures in the production of such meanings has received far less attention. They suggest that the structure of prestige—the cultural notions in terms of which one's value and worth are analyzed, and the processes by which this analysis takes place and affects one's prestige—may be just as important as the structure of marriage and kinship in most cultures, and perhaps more important in some, for an interpretation of sex and gender. Their discussion focuses more upon gender than upon sexual activity, and this emphasis is perhaps correct: sexual practice seems to be related to the structure of prestige through the crucial mediation of gender performance. One's prestige depends in part on one's ability to display in sufficient quantity culturally recognized gender characteristics, including those which concern sexual activity.

Gender is itself a prestige structure to the extent that prestige is allotted differently to men and women by virtue of their gender. Moreover, men often have more access than women to the roles to which prestige generally accrues. Beyond this point, however, Ortner and Whitehead argue that 'the concepts used to differentiate men from women in terms of social worth are often identical to the concepts used...to grade individuals of the same gender' (Ortner and Whitehead 1981: 16-17). In other words, the values in terms of which men are accorded more prestige than women are frequently the same values in terms of which some men are accorded more prestige than others.

Every culture has particular ideas about how men or women ought to act *as* men or women. These ideas extend not only to the sexual division of labor, but also to leisure activities, clothing, body language, and so forth. In North American culture, a phrase such as 'throwing like a girl' (cf. Young 1990: 141-59) easily conveys a certain image to most individuals, an image implanted through the socialization process. It triggers certain widely shared assumptions about the ways in which females (and, by implication through contrast, males) utilize their bodies and the space around their bodies in the manipulation of objects.

Attributes considered 'masculine' in a particular culture are often accorded a higher value than those considered 'feminine'. These attributes are then used not only to allot prestige differentially to men and women, but also to allot prestige differentially to particular men depending upon the degree of their own possession of said attributes. A good example is the 'active/passive' dichotomy. In many cultures, 'activity' is widely assumed to be a male trait and 'passivity' a female one. Yet the polar terms are also used to distinguish between men, so that a man who seems more 'passive' than 'active' often risks losing a certain amount of social prestige. The display of supposed feminine characteristics, like the display of masculine characteristics, can become a differentiating criterion not only between genders but also between different individuals possessing the same biological sex. It means one thing in American culture to say that a female 'throws like a girl', and quite another thing to say that a male does so. The implications of the phrase depend upon the biological sex of the person to whom the reference is made and the cultural assumptions about gender-specific behavior in the society in which the phrase is spoken.

While it is often assumed that males or females naturally 'act like men or women' by virtue of their biological sex, further reflection reveals that individuals of the same biological sex are actually quite varied in their demonstration of gender signals. It is this variation which allows members of a culture to evaluate individuals in terms of their possession of cultural gender signs. As Michael Herzfeld points out, in one of the villages which he studied it was not always as important to be 'a good man' as it was to be 'good at being a man' (Herzfeld 1985: 16). One can be successful or unsuccessful at displaying publicly and in sufficient quantity the appropriate (which is to say, appropriate within a particular culture) gender signals.

To fail to fulfill such cultural expectations is to leave oneself open to the charge of being an inadequate case of one's gender. For the man, this can amount to the charge of being 'feminine'; for the woman, of being 'masculine'. What must be grasped is the extent to which this accusation may affect one's prestige. For men in particular, 'masculinity' is often defined over against 'femininity', and prestige is granted primarily to the man who can demonstrate his possession of the former (see especially Gilmore 1987a; 1990). The situation of women is often similar but more ambiguous, since certain women who are perceived to 'act like a man' are admired rather than criticized (Blok 1981: 429; Brandes 1981: 231).

Sexual activities can play a crucial role in this semiotics of gender performance. The various ideas about 'how men act' and 'how women act' include, while extending far beyond, sexual practices. Individuals usually assume that there are certain ways in which the gendered subject (as well as, in some cases, the gendered object; cf. Lancaster 1988; 1992: 235-78) of sexual activity ought to act. A failure to meet these expectations in the realm of sexual practice impacts the overall estimate of one's prestige because it brings into question one's socially affirmed gender. Among men, for example, the omission or commission of a particular sexual act can raise questions about whether one is 'a real man'. For both men and women, sexual practice impacts the opinions held by others about a person's relation to 'natural' gender roles, and these opinions in turn affect that person's prestige.

However, even within a single culture, women and men may not hold the same ideas about prestige and its relation to gender and sexual practice. The criteria which women use to evaluate the social worth of men or of other women may or may not be identical to the criteria used by men to evaluate women or one another (cf. Wikan 1984; 1991; Moore 1988). Therefore, one should always inquire about the subject of this sort of evaluation, which is to say, the person or persons who carry it out. A discourse which betrays evidence of being primarily a discourse between men is more likely to utilize male assumptions about gender and prestige. Alternative assumptions that may exist among women of the same culture may not be represented in the sample case. Large segments, at least, of the biblical literature have been characterized as exactly such a male discourse (cf., for instance, Fewell and Gunn 1993; Exum 1993).

The implications of this line of anthropological thought for the interpretation of ancient texts are substantial. As noted above, readers or listeners tend to evaluate the actions of literary characters in terms of cultural norms. Authors assume that such evaluations take place, and so they exploit the possible effects that can be achieved by playing upon such cultural norms. When characters are specified as male or female, and hence gendered, one group of norms which will be utilized in the reading process is the set of gender norms held by the reader(s) in question. Any attempt to understand an ancient text in terms of its own contextual, conventional assumptions should examine the possible evaluation of characters in terms of ancient cultural gender norms. This step requires asking about the ways in which a gendered character fulfills or fails to fulfill culture-specific expectations about gender-specific behavior.

If gender and sexual practice are related to the structure of prestige, then the question of gender performance takes its place alongside other questions which biblical scholars routinely raise when attempting to understand how the status ascribed to a particular character affects the meaning of a text. We should not only recognize that a character does or does not meet the expectations of 'Levite', 'king', 'prophet' and so forth. We must also ask whether the character meets the expectations of 'male' and 'female', and base our interpretations of the possible meanings attributed to a character's actions accordingly. We must ask about the sort of context in which it could be meaningful for the Philistines to exhort one another to fight by using the simple refrain, 'Be men!' (1 Sam. 4.9), a phrase which implies the possibility that a certain course of action might result in their being shown to be, in some way, *less than* men (cf. also 1 Sam. 26.15). If sexual practice is one area in which such gendered behavior norms play a role, then stories in which sexual acts take place must be considered carefully in the light of gender-based prestige.

However, there is a problem here for the modern reader of ancient texts. How does one establish the content of the gender norms that might have been prevalent at the time and place from which these texts emerged? Unlike the anthropologists upon whose work Ortner and Whitehead rely, we are unable to observe directly the culture whose views we study.

One possible way to approach this question is through a further examination of more specific anthropological data. For example, one might seek particular configurations of cultural norms which seem to shed light on the biblical texts. One cultural complex considered especially useful by a number of scholars studying ancient (including biblical) texts is the complex referred to by the terms 'honor' and 'shame'.

Masculine Contest and Female Chastity
The ideological complex often referred to as the 'honor/shame' system of values is one prestige structure mentioned by Ortner and Whitehead. The anthropological literature on honor and shame in the Mediterranean basin and the Middle East has become relatively well known among biblical scholars, and all of its details do not need to be reviewed here. The issues raised in these discussions have already impacted the interpretation of ancient literature, from classical texts (Gouldner 1965; Winkler 1990) to the New Testament (Malina 1981; Neyrey [ed.] 1991) and from the literature of the Hebrew Bible (Bal 1988a; Matthews 1992; Matthews and Benjamin [eds.] 1993; Yee 1992) to such early Jewish texts as Ben Sira (Camp 1991). Anthropologists have themselves made

explicit links between the honor/shame complex, as it manifests itself in the cultures which they have studied, and certain ideological values that seem to underlie such ancient texts as the Homeric epics (see, for example, Gilmore 1990: 36-38; Campbell 1964: 263; cf. Finley 1978).

Much of the anthropological literature on honor and shame deals with societies along the northern shore of the Mediterranean Sea in such areas as Spain, Italy, Greece and Crete (see, for example, Brandes 1981; Herzfeld 1985; Giovannini 1987) and with societies along the southern shore in such areas as Morocco, Libya, and Algeria (see, for example, Bourdieu 1979; Davis 1987; Marcus 1987). However, a significant portion of the literature on honor and shame is based on societies in such Middle Eastern areas as Turkey, Jordan, Lebanon, Oman and Afghanistan (see, for example, Antoun 1968; Delaney 1987; 1991; Tapper 1991; Abu-Lughod 1986; Holy 1989; Wikan 1984; 1991). Indeed, certain cultural notions associated with the Mediterranean and Middle Eastern manifestations of honor and shame have been located in such distant locations as Nicaragua (Lancaster 1988; 1992) and Japan (Asano-Tamanoi 1987).

Because the anthropological literature on this topic is based on the study of such diverse cultures, it is unlikely that a single set of beliefs about honor and shame is equally relevant to all of the societies in question. Indeed, such differences as exist between the various local versions have been explicated through careful cross-cultural comparisons. If differences due to geographical separation can be found, then differences due to temporal separation can be assumed to exist as well. Thus, one must be cautious in using this anthropological material to interpret ancient texts, and such interpretations need to be based on literary analysis as well as cross-cultural comparison.

Nevertheless, while there is no single set of beliefs or approved cultural scenarios associated in every instance with honor and shame, one aspect of the system of values in question does appear in most of the relevant literature. That aspect is the relation between a competitive notion of masculine sexuality and an emphasis upon female chastity. This relation is used here as a heuristic lens for the examination of several biblical narratives in which both sexual contact and male conflicts are explicitly mentioned. Thus, the specific terms 'honor' and 'shame' are much less important for this study than the structural and symbolic relations around sex and gender that discussions of honor and shame have uncovered.

Sex and gender have long played a key role in debates about honor and shame (see, for example, Peristiany [ed.] 1965; Pitt-Rivers 1977).

Some anthropologists suggest that the early analysts of honor and shame stressed the sexual aspects of Mediterranean and Middle Eastern notions of 'honor' in a one-sided manner and neglected thereby other important components of honor such as honesty, cooperation, and especially hospitality (Herzfeld 1987; Gilmore 1987b). Nonetheless, David Gilmore, himself a critic of approaches that ignore these other qualities, has noted that the sexual element which recurs in the anthropological literature is one of the few cultural characteristics which does appear throughout much of the Mediterranean basin and parts of the Middle East, and which seems to be sufficiently widespread to justify treating the areas in question as a sort of unit (Gilmore 1987a; cf. Delaney 1987: 35).

In ethnographic accounts from various parts of the Mediterranean and the Middle East, one finds that women's sexuality is treated by indigenous men as a resource which, like other limited resources, can become the object of conflict. The point around which this conflict often coalesces is the chastity of women, which male kinsmen are compelled to guard with vigilance. The success with which a woman's sexual purity is maintained influences the social reputation of her male kinsmen (see Schneider 1971; Blok 1981; Giovannini 1981; 1987; Antoun 1968). The woman's own responsibility for her chastity seems to be variable; in at least some locations women are not considered capable of maintaining their sexual purity without the help of male relatives (see Delaney 1987; 1991).

The required vigilance of the woman's male relatives is itself justified by the belief in a competitive, predatory notion of masculine sexuality (Gilmore 1987a; 1990). One of the ways in which men can demonstrate their masculinity, at least in theory, is through sexual conquest. Sexual access to women, guarded ferociously by male kinsmen as a good which affects their own prestige, can sometimes be used by other men as a means with which to increase their prestige in turn. Since the honor of a woman's family is thought to depend in part upon the manner in which her kinsmen control access to her sexuality, sexual relations with the woman are a potential means of attack for a man who wishes to cast doubt upon that honor. By acquiring sexual access to the woman *in spite of* the wishes of her kinsmen, a man may hope to demonstrate that these kinsmen are incapable of the required vigilance. The man's sexual act can thus have the effect of negating the honor of the woman's kinsmen. Moreover, such an act may increase his own status in turn, provided that the act becomes known to others and is carried out in accordance with such additional protocols about sexual practice as may also exist in the society in question.

The sexual loyalty of a wife is thus an important determinant of a man's honor, and an unfaithful wife is particularly dreaded by men since her unfaithfulness has allowed another man to cast shame on her husband (Brandes 1981). The fact that the husband cannot always insure his wife's loyalty may produce the insecurity which seems to motivate the vehement denunciations of female promiscuity. In addition, the possibility that one's wife has been unfaithful raises a concern about the paternity of children born to her. Delaney (1991) argues that concern over paternity explains the emotion behind male obsessions with female chastity, since paternity, unlike maternity, is not self-evident.

However, the chastity of other women may be involved as well. For example, the virginity of sisters and daughters is frequently at stake in this sort of sexual contest (cf. Schneider 1971; Ortner 1978; Giovannini 1981; 1987), and brothers and fathers are often quite conscious of the need to protect family honor by guarding the sexual purity of their kinswomen. Indeed, this imperative can be experienced as a burden, as is indicated by one young male informant who, when asked why he and his brother would prefer not to have a sister, responded, 'Well, if we have a sister, Carlo and I will have to make sure no one calls her *puttana* [whore] or else our family will be laughed at' (Giovannini 1981: 408). This statement summarizes succinctly the role often played by female chastity in male struggles for personal and familial prestige, specifically, in this case, with regard to the sexual purity of sisters.

The implications which seem to concern the men in this framework are primarily those which impact themselves and other men. Aspersion on a woman's honor is important to her husband, her father, or her brothers because of the ways in which her sexual purity is tied to their own honor, and not because female honor as such, and apart from its impact upon male honor, is necessarily held by men in high esteem.[6]

---

6.   There is some disagreement in the anthropological literature about the nature of female honor. Certain influential discussions of honor and shame (for example, Pitt-Rivers 1977) imply that honor is associated especially with men while shame is associated especially with women. This opinion has been reproduced somewhat uncritically in biblical scholarship. Malina, for example, suggests that female honor is only relevant in contexts where women are considered as members of a group together with men. At the level of 'daily concrete behavior...honor is always male, and shame is always female' (1981: 45-6). However, Wikan (1984; 1991) argues

Gilmore notes that this structure triangulates the social relations involved. Sexual practice is not simply a matter of a single heterosexual couple. Rather,

> the masculine experience of sexuality becomes broadened conceptually to encompass a triad involving two men—or groups of men—and a woman, who is reduced to an intermediating object. Sexual relations are experienced as a measure of comparative virtue, judged as 'performance' among men. Necessarily, female sexuality becomes objectified, becoming not only a libidinal goal in itself, but a contentious and arbitrating social index for masculine reputation. (Gilmore 1987a: 4-5)

Two points emerge from this statement. First, the emphasis upon masculine reputation indicates that the reputation in question is that of the man *as a man*. In other words, it is masculinity itself, within a certain economy of gender, that is at stake. Both the kinsman and the potential sexual partner can demonstrate their ability to embody a particular sort of manhood by their actions in preventing or accomplishing sexual contact with the woman. Public awareness of a sexual act can affect the prestige of both men in this way.

Secondly, it is uncertain whether the more ideologically charged relation here is actually that between the man and the woman, or rather that between the men. To be sure, the woman and her sexuality are a crucial part of the picture. However, it is doubtful that the importance accorded to her sexuality *by the men* can be registered apart from a consideration of its possible impact upon male–male relations. From the perspective of the men who share this set of assumptions, the relations between men are at least as important for the meanings attached to heterosexual contact as the relation between the men and the woman. It is this fact which raises the notion of the 'traffic in women'.

Before discussing this latter notion, it should be noted that any attempt to capitalize upon the ideological links between male sexual predation, male honor, and female purity can be a hazardous enterprise. Additional norms and beliefs about sexual practice and honor, apart from those just discussed, inevitably exist in a given society, and so the indigenous subject who chooses this course of action always risks contravening some other cultural norm in the process. A sexual act carried

that these perceptions result from the fact that male anthropologists often rely on male informants and therefore reproduce male bias. Among themselves women may believe in individual female honor, and the criteria for this honor can differ from the criteria for male honor (cf. Goddard 1987; Lindisfarne 1994).

out by a man with a woman who is associated with his male rival might in theory bring honor upon the male sexual subject and shame upon the other man. In practice, however, other factors need to be taken into consideration as well. If, for example, the male rival in question is one's own father, whom one ought always to honor, or a political subordinate, in relation to whom the unbridled exercise of power can appear not as a challenge but rather as an abuse, then the impact upon one's prestige might turn out to be negative rather than positive. These sorts of complexities indicate that we should not think of the norms involved here as absolute laws and customs, but rather as a web of symbolic associations that an actor must be able to manipulate strategically and with prudence when confronting all sorts of variable situations. Several discussions of honor and shame (for instance, Lindisfarne 1994; Bourdieu 1977) underscore this complexity. Thus, when interpreting texts in the light of these associations, we must always consider the possibility that the plot of the story is built upon the tension among various cultural norms which potentially conflict with one another in practice.

The 'Traffic in Women' and Male Social Relations

The term 'traffic in women' is taken from an influential essay by Gayle Rubin (1975) which attempts to analyze some of the structural underpinnings of the dominance of men over women. In the course of a wide-ranging discussion, Rubin produces insightful readings of, among others, Marx, Engels, Freud and Lacan. It is primarily her reading of Claude Lévi-Strauss and his theories of kinship, however, which will concern us here.

Lévi-Strauss tried to account for what he considered the near-universal presence of the incest taboo, which however assumed different forms in different societies and, hence, could not be considered a simple reflection of 'natural' realities (Lévi-Strauss 1969). Lévi-Strauss argued that the real function of incest taboos can be found in the resulting imperative for men to marry women who are members of another kinship group. This imperative enforces the exchange of women between groups of men. Interpreting this exchange in the light of Mauss's theory of the gift (see Mauss 1990; cf. Sahlins 1972: 149-230), Lévi-Strauss suggested that the result of the exchange is a network of social alliances which holds kinship societies together. He further suggested that the incest taboo and the exchange of women which it enforces constitute the very origin and foundation of culture; they bring into existence the alliances upon which society necessarily depends.

Rubin is understandably critical of this last notion since it entails the implicit corollary that culture cannot exist without the subordination of women. Nevertheless, she insists that Lévi-Strauss's analysis is useful, not as an explanation for the origin of culture per se, but rather as a tool for understanding the symbolic logic of many societies in which women are subordinate to men (cf. Mitchell 1974: 370-76). One presupposition of this logic is that men have the right to be agents of the exchange of women, while women are often reduced to the status of exchange objects. Thus, men establish and negotiate their relations with one another through their relations with women. Women, though important to the process, serve as 'a conduit of a relationship' between men (Rubin 1975: 174).

Rubin's essay, grounded as it is in an 'exegetical' analysis of Lévi-Strauss, focuses on marriage and kinship as the most significant points in the exchange system. However, she suggests that not only relations of alliance but also relations of conflict might be expressed in terms of the logic of the 'traffic in women'. Regina Schwartz has articulated this particular point well by suggesting that 'when women are stolen, rather than peaceably exchanged, the relational directions reverse, from friendship toward fear, from alliance toward hostility' (Schwartz 1991: 47).

Rubin does not limit the significance of the concept of the 'traffic in women' to the particular societies which Lévi-Strauss analyzed in his studies of kinship, but suggests instead that the same general principle appears in many different societies.[7] Understood broadly, the symbolic connotations of Rubin's notion of a 'traffic in women' cohere well with the other elements of my interpretive frame. If prestige and gender are related, albeit in a number of different ways, then this relationship has effects both upon men's relations with women and also upon men's relations with other men. A man's relations with women can be seen from the perspective of the male actor in terms of the possible impact of those relations upon male prestige. The range of possibilities is quite broad, as Ortner and Whitehead (1981: 21) indicate:

---

7.   In her 1975 essay Rubin suggests that even modern industrial societies can be analyzed in terms of the 'traffic in women'. However, in a later article (1984), she states that her earlier analysis cannot be applied in a straightforward manner to industrial societies in which kinship does not play a significant structuring role. The relevance of her original argument for the present project does not seem to be affected by this modification, since kinship does seem to have played a significant structuring role in the culture which produced the Hebrew Bible, and indeed in the text itself.

[M]ale prestige is deeply involved in cross-sex relations. Women may be cast as the prize for male prowess or success; having a wife may be the prerequisite to full adult male status; good or bad liaisons with women may raise or lower one's status; the status of one's mother may systematically affect one's status at birth; the sexual comportment of one's sisters and daughters may polish or dull one's honor; and so forth.

If these and other relations with women can affect male prestige vis-à-vis other men, then it is likely that men often manipulate their relations with females to achieve particular goals in the realm of their relations with other men. Indeed, the notion of a 'traffic in women' may extend far beyond the relatively clear example of marriage alliances. All sorts of male–female relations can be interrogated for what they tell us about all sorts of male–male relations. Sexual relations are potentially one case of a much larger set. In regard to any particular heterosexual contact, we can ask not only whether it violates or adheres to dominant ethical norms about sexual activity. We must at least raise the question of whether the act reveals anything about a male–male relation—whether, that is to say, the woman involved in the sexual contact is serving as the 'conduit of a relationship', in Rubin's words, between two men. If there is evidence that such is the case, then the exact nature of the relationship should be analyzed.

There are certainly limits to the answers provided by an analysis in terms of the male 'traffic in women'. Since the concept is useful precisely as a means of understanding the symbolic role of women in relations between men, the women in question are visible primarily in terms of their function within male ideology, a fact of which Rubin herself is well aware. Consequently, the actual perspectives or agency of the women themselves tend to remain invisible in the analysis (cf. Sedgwick 1985: 18). It is therefore crucial to distinguish once again between the views of and about women in the biblical text, on the one hand, and the actual views of real Israelite women, on the other hand, which may or may not cohere in a given instance. Rubin's analysis as a critical tool will be most helpful with regard to the former, but perhaps less helpful with regard to the latter.

Conclusion

The various areas of anthropological discussion which I have outlined here will be utilized as a frame for the readings of biblical stories offered in Chapter 4. I will attempt to show that, by examining the texts in the light of these anthropological themes, it is possible to construct a 'thick interpretation' which can account for the words and actions of biblical characters by relating them to a network of cultural presuppositions and symbolic associations.

The term 'thick interpretation' is chosen advisedly in this context. 'Thick interpretation' calls to mind Geertz's notion of 'thick description' as a valuable enterprise in which the anthropologist attempts to describe and elaborate upon the webs of symbolic meaning that constitute a particular culture (Geertz 1973: 3-30). Yet I have intentionally substituted the word 'interpretation' for 'description' in order to account for the crucial fact that biblical scholars cannot proceed in quite the manner that Geertz proposes for his anthropological colleagues. Geertz, himself quite sensitive to the interpretive nature of anthropological discourse, can nevertheless rely upon a certain amount of empirical observation as ground for his 'thick description'. As Meyers (1988: 13) points out, '*empirical* observation of various social circumstances and relationships is not possible' for the scholar of ancient Israelite culture. Particularly in a project such as the present one, where literary texts rather than the observed actions of a culture are subjected to analysis, one must acknowledge that any social or cultural analysis proceeds by way of *reading*. Consequently, one must be more specific about the manner in which the analysis of a piece of literary discourse is carried out, as well as the way in which one understands the relationship between a literary discourse and cultural assumptions. This problem is addressed in the next chapter.

Chapter 3

A NARRATOLOGICAL METHOD OF ANALYSIS

The use of a specific method of literary analysis, which can be described and utilized for the purposes of an intersubjective discussion and evaluation of textual interpretations, is an essential safeguard against implausible anthropological readings: it forces interpreters to consider particular textual features, to incorporate those features into the interpretation, and to communicate to their audience some idea about the ways in which this process takes place. The present chapter examines a narratological model of textual analysis developed by the Dutch literary theorist Mieke Bal. Bal's approach to narrative texts has a particularly attractive feature for the present project inasmuch as she devotes some attention to the relations between literary analysis and the question of cultural context. Indeed, Bal claims that her narratological method is able 'to establish connections between textual features and social meanings' with more facility than most methods of literary analysis (Bal 1988b: 32). Therefore, some attention will be given to her theoretical and practical work on the use of anthropology in textual interpretation.

The discussion presented here is by no means a complete summary or analysis of Bal's work. On the contrary, even her work on biblical literature is treated only in terms of the aspects which seem most helpful for the present project. Following her own suggestion, I will consider narratology as a 'tool' (Bal 1985: x) for textual interpretation, a tool which has its own specific advantages and disadvantages.

A Narratological Method of Analysis

The term 'narratology' emerged from formalist and structuralist attempts to develop a 'poetics' of narrative literature. By 'poetics', narrative analysts usually mean a body of analytic discourse which stands to narrative literature in roughly the same relationship that linguistics stands to language (cf. Culler 1975; 1981: 169-87; Todorov 1977; Chatman

1978; Genette 1980; Rimmon-Kenan 1983; Prince 1982; W. Martin 1986; and in Hebrew Bible studies, Berlin 1983). In many ways Bal's narratology fits into this tradition of narrative theory. However, Bal articulates an explicitly 'instrumental view' of narratology, conceived not only as an account of narrative discourse in general but also as a tool for the interpretation of specific texts (Bal 1985: ix-x; 9-10).[1] At its most basic, Bal's method consists of an analysis of texts[2] in terms of three narrative activities: action, focalization, and speech. Simply put, the analysis of these activities entails an examination of the implications of three questions: Who acts? Who sees? and Who speaks? (Bal 1989: 17). These questions in turn imply a whole series of further analytical questions, the asking and answering of which constitute the core of Bal's narratological method.

The formulation of these three initial questions ('*Who* acts? *Who* sees? *Who* speaks?') implies an agent or agents for each activity. Bal most often refers to the agents in question as the *subjects* of the narrative activities (Who is the subject of action? Who is the subject of focalization? Who is the subject of speech?). This way of referring to the agents of narrative discourse has the advantage of implying the possible existence of objects as well, as we shall see.

By raising the question 'Who acts?', Bal calls attention to an area of narrative discourse that has traditionally served as the focal point for structuralist studies: the events that take place and the actors associated with those events. Bal refers to the analysis of these elements of narrative discourse as the analysis of the 'fabula', a term adopted from Russian formalism.[3] She defines a fabula as 'a series of logically and

1. Other narratologists recognize that the division between poetics and interpretation is a relative one and that there is a dialectical relationship between the two endeavours (cf., for example, Todorov 1977: 35-36; Genette 1980: 21-23). However, some narratologists resist the attempt 'to make of narratology primarily an aid to interpretation' (Prince 1988: 357).

2. Bal explicitly states that narratology can be profitably utilized in the study of non-narrative texts as well as texts traditionally classified as narratives (cf., for example, Bal 1985: 7; 1990b: 730; 1991b). This belief is related to her contention that 'narrative' refers most usefully not to a specific class of texts, the members of which could theoretically be specified, but rather to 'a discursive mode which affects semiotic objects in variable degrees' (1990b: 730). Her most recent work (1991b; 1994: 109-303) includes narratological analyses of paintings.

3. On Russian formalism, see Matejka and Pomorska (eds.) 1971; Todorov 1977: 247-67.

chronologically related events that are caused or experienced by actors'
(Bal 1985: 5).

The study of events, actors, and the relations between them is a basic
component of narrative analysis. However, Bal attempts to make her
analytical method more subtle in several ways. For example, she refuses
to divide characters simply into the two classes of those who have access
to the position of acting subject and those who do not. She points out
that characters denied access to subject-positions can still play a role,
sometimes an important role, in the development of a narrative: they can
become objects of the actions of other characters, and the events which
result can be important for the subsequent narrative development. To
illustrate this point, Bal calls attention to the women taken as wives by
the Israelites in the book of Judges:

> [T]he women do not act either; they are not subjects but objects of action,
> typically given away or taken. Within the fabula as a series of events,
> however, the event of which they are the objects, does have conse-
> quences…it triggers the following episode…Hence, if it is true that the
> women have no subject-position at all, their relevance as elements in the
> story has to be assessed. (Bal 1988b: 33)

Moreover, characters who act and who might therefore be classified
as subjects of narrative action may on closer analysis turn out to be
acting only in response to the actions of another character (for example,
following the order of a king) or within certain constraints. Thus, one
must consider the extent to which subject-positions with regard to action
can be correlated with social differentials (ruler vs. ruled, Israelite vs.
non-Israelite, male vs. female, and so on). The effect of a narrative
depends in part upon the correlations established between narrative
subject-positions and social differentials.

It should already be apparent that, far from simplifying the structure
of a narrative or leading unproblematically to its 'correct' interpretation,
Bal's questions indicate just how complex narrative discourse actually is,
and they indicate as well a means of penetrating this complexity. Indeed,
still more questions can be generated from the initially simple question,
'Who acts?', questions such as the following:

> Do each of the characters act in their turn, or are some characters only
> acted upon?…is their action physical or only mental; is it integrated within
> the network of the overall fabula, or does it seem isolated?…Is the
> grammatical subject of the sentence the causal subject of the action? (Bal
> 1988b: 36)

As nuanced as Bal's handling of the question 'Who acts?' becomes, her handling of the question 'Who sees?' is even more complicated. This question is related to the concept of focalization, a concept used by some narratologists but only recently (and partly due to Bal's influence) employed by biblical scholars (see, for example, Exum 1993).

The concept of focalization is related to Bal's distinction between 'fabula' and 'story'. We have already seen that Bal employs 'fabula' to refer to the series of events that make up a narrative and to the actors associated with those events. When we read or hear a 'story', however, those events and those actors are presented to us in a particular fashion. The story, in which events and actors are represented in a certain manner, can be differentiated from the fabula, which is a theoretical entity made up of those same events and actors prior to their manipulation into a particular structure of representation.

The difference between fabula and story is perhaps best explained in terms of the question of narrative order. Events recounted in a narrative text are not always recounted in the same order in which, logically, we know that they must have occurred. For example, in one of the texts examined in the next chapter, 2 Sam. 3.7, we read that 'Saul had a concubine and her name was Rizpah'. By the time we are given this information, Saul is, within the world of the narrative, already dead. Logically, we know that the relationship between Saul and Rizpah was established prior to the point at which we are first told about it; a distinction clearly exists here between a logical order in which events can be assumed to have happened (1. Saul has a concubine named Rizpah, 2. Saul dies) and another order, the order in which events are recounted in the text (1. Saul dies, 2. Saul has a concubine named Rizpah).[4]

Such a distinction is one of several that the analyst makes in order to differentiate fabula from story. In this example, the fabula consists of the events in the order in which we assume they must logically have happened. When these events are represented in such a fashion that this order changes, the layer of the fabula shifts to the layer of the story. A

4.   A narratological reference to an event having 'happened' is concerned strictly with an event having taken place in the world of the narrative. Claims about the actual historical occurrence of these events in ancient Israel are neither implied nor denied, and they would need to be evaluated on the basis of criteria other than those supplied by narratology. This is not to say that historiographic texts cannot be analyzed with narratological tools, but rather that such tools are designed to answer specific questions.

certain number of elements, including not only events which take place in some logical order but also actors and locations, are 'organized in a certain way into a story' (Bal 1985: 7). We can reconstruct the fabula logically and for analytic purposes on the basis of our understanding of the story. The story is the result of a certain way of rendering the fabula, a way of rendering it which achieves its effects by representing the elements of the fabula in this manner rather than that, with these emphases rather than those, in this order rather than another. Charting the course from fabula to story is thus a way of examining the specific literary strategies of a given text, and presupposes that the same fabula could have been presented in an altogether different manner.

Here a note of caution about terminology is in order. The concepts involved here have entered the English language in a number of different forms (cf. Toolan 1988: 11). For example, Bal's distinction between 'fabula' and 'story' is roughly parallel to Seymour Chatman's distinction between 'story' and 'discourse' (Chatman 1978: 19). Yet the English word 'story' in these two theories refers to different objects: Bal's 'fabula' is more or less equivalent to Chatman's 'story', while Bal's 'story' is somewhat similar to Chatman's 'discourse'. Since Chatman's theory has had a certain amount of influence,[5] one should be clear about the referent of each term within the scope of the particular theory being used. To be consistent, I will utilize Bal's terminology throughout this analysis.[6]

The concept of focalization is for Bal a crucial element of the manipulation of a fabula into a story. It deals with the fact that, in a story, we 'see' the elements of the fabula only by way of the particular manner in which they are represented for us. Our vision of the fabula is mediated by a complex structure of representation. The analysis of this mediation is approached with the help of the concept of 'focalization'.

The term 'focalization' entered the lexicon of narratology through the work of Gerard Genette. By discussing focalization Genette hoped to clarify what he called 'a confusion between the question *Who is the*

5.   See, for example, the work of Culpepper (1983) which relies heavily on Chatman's work.

6.   Partly because of such difficulties it seems preferable to me to employ a single model of narrative discourse, specifically Bal's model, which can be explained and then used consistently in my textual analyses, rather than appealing to a potpourri of narrative theorists whose theories are often different from or incompatible with one another.

character whose point of view orients the narrative perspective? and the very different question *who is the narrator?*—or, more simply, the question *who sees?* and the question *who speaks?*' (Genette 1980: 186, emphasis in original). Genette pointed out that, in principle, the narrator of a text need not be the locus of the narrative perspective, which might instead be placed with a particular character.

Bal herself defines focalization as 'the relationship between the vision, the agent that sees, and that which is seen' (Bal 1985: 104). This definition moves beyond Genette by specifying the subject- and object-positions involved in focalization: each instance of focalization, each time something is 'seen' in a story by the audience or by one of the characters, involves both a 'focalizer' or subject of focalization ('the agent that sees') and a 'focalized' or object of focalization ('that which is seen'). These specifications can be used to derive certain questions as starting points for the analysis of focalization in any particular narrative text, including for example the following three questions (Bal 1985: 106, emphasis in original):

1.   *What* does the character focalize: what is it aimed at?
2.   *How* does it do this: with what attitude does it view things?
3.   *Who* focalizes it: whose focalized object is it?

When we ask *who* focalizes, we are asking about the subject of the vision contained within the narrative. Do we see the events along with the narrator, or through the eyes of a specific character? When we ask about the *attitude* with which the subject focalizes, we are dealing with the question of ideology. This question is not restricted in Bal's theory to content-analysis but necessarily includes a subtle analysis of the specific ways in which a text can manipulate its readers. Focalization is, in Bal's opinion, of primary importance here (cf. Bal 1985: 116-17). When we ask '*what* does the character (or narrator) focalize', we are asking about the object of the vision, about that which is 'seen' either literally or figuratively.

These questions, when put to any particular text, can again yield a series of further questions that impact our interpretation of the text. For example, when events and characters are presented in a certain fashion, we can ask not only about the subject of the presentation, but also about possible alternative subject-positions that are not represented in the text. If we wish to understand how the structure of a text contributes to our interpretation of its meaning, it is just as important, and perhaps even more important, to ask 'Who is *not* given access to the position of focalizing subject?' as it is to ask 'Who is the subject of focalization?' A fabula presented in terms of a different focalization might result in a quite different story, in spite of the fact that the same events and actors are involved.

For example, the fabula of the book of Joshua includes a series of events such as 1. the Israelites enter Canaan, 2. the Israelites march around the city of Jericho, 3. the walls of Jericho fall, and 4. the Israelites kill the inhabitants of Jericho, with the exception of Rahab and her family, at the command of the Israelite deity. One characteristic of the text in which these events are recounted is the fact that they are presented primarily from points of view sympathetic to YHWH and the Israelites. There is, for example, no recording of the perspective of the inhabitants of Jericho at the moment at which the Israelites enter the city and begin destroying its citizens. To grasp the significance of this fact, we need only to imagine a rendering of the same series of events, as focalized by the inhabitants of Jericho (for example, 'the people of Jericho watched in horror as the invading foreigners began killing men, women, and children without mercy at the command of their bloodthirsty deity'). Needless to say, such a rendering would result in an altogether different 'story', in the sense given this term by Bal, in spite of the fact that the fabula is the same. We can only imagine how provocative a thoroughly 'Canaanite' version of the stories found in Genesis–2 Kings, which is to say, a recounting of the same events but focalized by 'Canaanites', would be.[7]

One reason why Bal prefers the concept of focalization to the more traditional 'point of view' is that it can help us avoid the suggestion that a text necessarily contains only a single perspective. There may be a single overriding point of view which orients a particular narrative, but even when this is the case (as it often is in biblical literature), alternative perspectives can be 'embedded' in the text (cf. Bal 1981a). In other words, just as the narrator, the 'first speaker' of a text, can turn the position of speaking subject over to a character (see below), so also the

---

7.   For a justification of the quotation marks around 'Canaanite', see the important study by Lemche (1991). A thorough *narratological* examination of the biblical representations of relations between Israelites and 'Canaanites' might yield significant results in the area of ideological analysis, and the concept of focalization could play a crucial role in such a study. Lemche's work is already a significant step in that direction (see especially pp. 101-21).

'first focalizer' can turn the position of focalizing subject over to a character, and the content of this focalization may conflict with the focalization of other characters or may not cohere with the overall perspective of the text. Since the analysis of focalization asks about the specific subject of focalization in each individual case, it may be a more precise tool for analyzing the ways in which a text achieves its effects than approaches which ask only about *the* point of view of a text.

Attention to the question of the subject of focalization also forces us to notice the interpretations of the actions of some characters by other characters in the course of a narrative. The effect of a narrative can only be analyzed when we interpret the *semiotic interaction between actors represented in the text.* These actors can see and evaluate the words and actions of other characters, which is to say, they can function as subjects of focalization; the particular ways in which this happens in a given text constitute part of that text's literary technique (cf. Bal 1981b: 203-206). We interpret the significance of actors and events in part as a result of the interpretations characters make of one another. This phenomenon is rather frequent in biblical narrative and it raises specific problems for the modern reader inasmuch as the social presuppositions of the interpretations one character make of another's actions are not always apparent.

The question 'Who speaks?' enables us to approach two distinct but related groups of narratological questions concerning the narrator on the one hand and direct or indirect discourse on the other. Bal defines a 'narrative text' as 'a text in which a narrative agent tells a story'. This narrative agent is the 'narrator', which Bal understands as 'the linguistic subject, a function and not a person, which expresses itself in the language that constitutes the text' (Bal 1985: 119). The narrator is not identical to the actual author(s) of the text, since it is a linguistic function only. It is the primary subject of speech in a narrative text, the linguistic 'voice' heard from the beginning of the story.

Although a narrator tells the story, in doing so it can yield the floor to another speaking agent which stands, as it were, on a separate level below that of the narrator (cf. Bal 1985: 134-42; 1991a: 86-91). Within the discourse of the narrator, one can find recounted the speech of another speaking agent. This well-known possibility produces the phenomenon of 'direct discourse': the narrator turns the position of subject of speech over to another agent, a character, who can in theory yield to yet another character whose discourse is embedded in the discourse of the first character, and so on.

Thus, one must determine which characters actually function as speaking subjects in a given narrative. By implication, one must also determine which characters do not function as speaking subjects. Whose speech do we hear, and whose speech is never made available to us? Once again we need to ask whether the answers to these questions can be related to the status and social positions of the characters. To use as an example a question which plays a central role in Bal's own analyses: does it seem that access to the position of speaking subject is allowed more often for characters of one gender than another? In what sorts of situations are exceptions made? The answers can have crucial implications for the effects which the narrative has upon us, and for the possible meanings which we attribute to it.

When examining the layer of speech and narration, one can also analyze the *modes* of speech that are utilized (Bal 1991a: 161; cf. Bar-Efrat 1989: 64-77). We can consider, for example, whether dialogue or monologue tends to predominate in a certain text, or even in the speech of a particular character; whether certain characters tend to ask questions and others provide answers; and whether there is a pattern to the distribution of 'request and demand...imperative and interrogative' (Bal 1988b: 35). Our impression of the characters can be impacted by such factors. For example, monologue could conceivably contribute to the impression that a particular character is dictatorial, or has/claims to have direct access to some higher (for instance, divine) authority. Similarly, the assignment of question and response to particular characters may contribute to our interpretation. As Bal points out, 'Questions assume a distribution of knowledge: the one who asks the question does not have knowledge, whereas the interlocuter is supposed to know' (Bal 1991a: 160). These sorts of questions only begin to disclose possibilities for the sorts of analytical questions that can be taken into consideration with regard to narration and speech in the interpretive process.

Access to textual meaning is mediated by the interaction of these various narrative subjects: the subjects of action, the subjects of focalization, and the subjects of speech. A narratological method allows us to analyze an instance of narrative discourse in light of the recognition that such discourse 'is specific in its structuring, through the staging of a variety of subjects, of a multiple, heterogeneous bundle of semiotic acts' (Bal 1994: 21). Our interpretations of narrative texts result from our own interaction with the 'subjectal network' (Bal 1991a: 160) of a text, the particular configuration of subject-positions that exists at any given point in the narrative with regard to the activities of speaking, focalizing, and acting.

By using an analysis of narrative subjects as a starting point for interpretation, we are able to link our interpretation to specific textual features. Pragmatically speaking, our ability to appeal to particular elements of the text as we put forth an interpretation of that text helps to establish the plausibility of the reading (cf. Bal 1987: 10-36). This fact is particularly important for an approach which makes use of questions derived from cross-cultural comparison. By encouraging the analyst to account for textual structures, narratological questions can hold in check (without removing entirely) the problem of circular analysis raised by critics of comparativism.[8]

However, Bal does not defend her narratological method by claiming that it will result in the one true meaning of a text. On the contrary, she recognizes that 'interpretation, although not absolutely arbitrary since it does, or should, interact with a text, is in practice unlimited and free' (Bal 1985: x). This statement reflects an interactionist position on the question of meaning that recurs throughout her work. On the one hand, Bal quite explicitly asserts that meanings of texts require 'the active participation of readers or listeners for their existence' (Bal 1988a: 135). Indeed, she has been criticized (by, for instance, Alter [1989: 221-27]) for granting too much freedom to the reader in the attribution of textual meaning. Her utilization of structuralist-inspired models is neither part of a quest for quasi-scientific certainty nor a denial of the role of the reader in the production of meaning. On the other hand, she insists that there are empirical features of narrative discourse which can be identified, analyzed, and discussed; that criteria for evaluating the relative plausibility of different readings can be articulated (even if we admit that such criteria are largely conventional [cf. Bal 1987: 11-15]); and that there is such a thing as 'good reading' which can be contrasted with 'obviously bad reading' (Bal 1991a: 11). Such statements demonstrate her recognition of the input of text *and* reader in the production of meaning.

For Bal, narratology helps to supply tools for negotiating the interactions between reader and text. It provides a series of questions to ask

8.   For an influential critique of comparativism by a biblical scholar, see Talmon 1978. I am more optimistic than Talmon about the value of cross-cultural comparisons for biblical interpretation. However, my insistence that such comparisons are best carried out in relation to a close reading of literary texts is an attempt to recognize the importance of the issues raised by Talmon and others.

about a text and a discourse with which to communicate to others both our interpretation and the ways in which we have gone about constructing it. Yet narratology, while in her view a necessary tool, is by no means a sufficient one. Bal recognizes that there are limits to narratology, questions that arise during the reading of a narrative which narratology cannot answer. One limit to which she draws particular attention is the boundary between narrative on the one hand and social history and/or anthropology on the other.

Anthropology and a Narratological Analysis

The usefulness of Bal's work for the present project does not lie exclusively in her narratological method. Bal also emphasizes the value of anthropology for the interpretation of ancient texts (see, for instance, Bal 1988a: 51-73; 1988b; 1990b; 1990c). Her remarks on anthropology as a tool for literary critics are actually rather extensive, and they make up an important area of her work which has not been sufficiently explored by biblical scholars.

Bal suggests that her narratological method is most productive precisely when its limits—and hence the need for contributions from other disciplines—are recognized. Once the limits of narratology have been reached, insights derived from other disciplines must be utilized if one does not wish to 'close off' (Bal 1988b: 39) the interpretation prematurely (cf. Bal 1988a). In *Death and Dissymmetry*, for example, Bal states that the 'two opposing boundaries that the narratological analysis [of the book of Judges] will hit are philology on the textual side and anthropology and history on the social side' (1988b: 39). The existence of these boundaries necessitates an interdisciplinary reading. Her argument that philological work is a necessary component of biblical interpretation is unlikely to meet with dissent.[9] Her insistence as a literary critic on the value of an anthropological perspective is much more

---

9.   Biblical scholars are likely to raise questions about Bal's specific philological conclusions, however (cf., for example, Brettler 1990: 100; Boyarin 1990: 37). The questions that have been raised about, for instance, Bal's use of Hebrew prepositions are important ones; even David Jobling, probably Bal's most ardent defender to date among biblical scholars, acknowledges the problem (Jobling 1991b). However, discussion of such difficulties lies outside the present project, which is concerned with Bal's literary theory and narratological method and not her philological work.

significant, for newer approaches in biblical literary criticism seldom take anthropological material into account.[10]

Bal voices a concern about literary approaches which avoid addressing the social dimensions of texts; she criticizes, for example, what she sees as the 'excessive aestheticizing approach' of a scholar such as Fokkelman (Bal 1988b: 260). Bal does recognize the difficulties involved in reading a text while taking into account its relationship to social reality. However, she also recognizes that textual meaning actually involves two different sorts of reading: our reading of the text, and the text's reading of the world or 'pre-text' which exists prior to it and to which the text itself is a sort of reaction:

> [T]he text, as produced by its author, responds to and brings order into the collection of possible meanings couched in…the pre-text. The pre-text is the historical, biographical, and ideological reality from which the text emerges…The second moment of meaning occurs when the reader formulates an ordering and reworking of the collection of possible meanings offered by the text…The author reflects upon the pre-text, and the reader reflects upon that text which is his or her pre-text. Both subjects [i.e. the author and the reader] are directed by the conventions of reading of their time and social group, and by their own historical position. (Bal 1989: 14)

Given this account of the production of textual meaning, we can state the role of anthropology in the reading process as follows: anthropological information helps the reader generate hypotheses about the pretext to which a particular text can plausibly be read as having responded and with which the text can plausibly be read as having interacted. This pre-text need not be limited to material or political facts, but may also include ideological conventions and symbolic meanings, as will primarily be the case in the next chapter.

To be sure, reconstructions of the reading of a socio-historical pre-text by a biblical author involve substantial hypothesis and conjecture. In some cases we have very little access to the process apart from its result, which is the text that lies before us. Thus, our claims about the readings performed by the author(s) are related to our own readings and involve our own particular subjectivity. Archaeologists and scholars of ancient history and literature are often able to provide relevant information about the pre-text of the Hebrew Bible, though the nature of the relationship

---

10. The lack of dialogue between literary approaches to biblical interpretation and approaches that make use of the social sciences has often been noted. For a recent discussion, see Segovia 1995; cf. Jobling 1990; 1991a.

between these fields and the study of the biblical texts continues to be debated and raises additional problems of interpretation (cf., for example, Dever 1990: 3-36; Coote and Whitelam 1987: 11-26; Meyers 1988: 16-23; Jamieson-Drake 1991). However, archaeology is often more useful for a reconstruction of the *material* pre-text interpreted or presupposed by an author than it is for a reconstruction of the *symbolic or ideological* pre-text.[11]

For Bal, the gesture of contextualizing the production of a text is nevertheless an important one, and her reasons for insisting upon this fact appear to be related to her appreciation of the strengths of anthropology as a discipline. Speaking retrospectively about her work on the Hebrew Bible, Bal notes 'the usefulness of... integrating an anthropological eagerness for understanding real otherness with a narratological method of structural textual analysis' (Bal 1990b: 733). This stance of 'eagerness for understanding real otherness' is the hallmark of anthropology, at least in theory, and Bal recognizes that such a stance is valuable when one approaches the Hebrew Bible, 'which poses a number of acute problems of alterity' (Bal 1990b: 733). The alterity results from the cultural gap which exists between our world, in which we necessarily exist as investigating subjects, and the world out of which the Hebrew Bible emerged. The danger to be avoided here, at least to the extent that such avoidance is possible, is the traditional anthropological problem of *ethnocentrism*: the tendency to interpret and evaluate facts about another culture in terms of the ideological framework and scale of values characteristic of our own.

According to Bal, this danger is nowhere more acute than in the investigation of gender. Much of her work on Judges centers around the possibility that terms dealing with female status have been wrongly understood and/or translated by readers who interpret these terms within the specific framework of their own culture-specific (and sometimes gender-specific) beliefs. To delineate this situation, she refers to Clifford Geertz's influential essay, 'From the Native's Point of View' (in Geertz 1983: 55-70), the interpretive moves of which she sees as exhibiting parallels to her study of Judges:

> My first response to these problems was, let's say, 'anthropological'. For
> just as Geertz became suspicious in the face of a concept [of the individual

---

11. I do not wish to imply that material and symbolic pre-texts are not related. For an excellent attempt to explore connections between material and symbolic factors, see McNutt 1990; cf. Flanagan 1988; Meyers 1988.

human subject] so central to Western culture...and rightly set out to challenge its universal validity, so did I become suspicious before the conjunction of these...concepts indicating female status in a culture we have reason to assume was thoroughly patriarchal, but which were translated into modern patriarchal terms. In other words, these translations seemed to endorse too smoothly the notion that patriarchy is a monolithic, transhistorical social form. (Bal 1990b: 734)

Bal draws an analogy here between the healthy suspicion of the anthropologist and the healthy suspicion of the biblical critic. The anthropologist assumes as a methodological starting point that our tendency is to assimilate practices and beliefs of other cultures to our own social framework. Similarly, Bal believes that the biblical critic ought to assume as a methodological starting point that our tendency is to assimilate practices and beliefs represented in the biblical texts, and hence presupposing some socially based web of meanings, to our own modern, Western social framework. Indeed, this problem would seem to be compounded for the biblical critic, since both space *and time* separate us from the culture(s) whose texts we wish to understand. Ethnocentrism and anachronism go hand in hand.

The problem of cultural distance can never be eliminated, even with the help of an anthropological approach. However, the difficulty of the task need not lead us to discard the attempt to understand the cultural assumptions of texts from another time and place. Bal points out that the effects of a methodological refusal to acknowledge the alien cultural framework of biblical texts can be serious. Minimizing the cultural otherness of the text, we all the more easily project upon it, as *the* meaning of the text, what are in fact beliefs and prejudices specific to our own society.[12] While an anthropological approach cannot eliminate this problem, it can help to mitigate its more pernicious manifestations:

Not that the anthropological codes by definition protect the researcher from closure, anachronism, ethnocentrism, and androcentrism...But the fact remains that the anthropological project stimulates a *critical attitude* toward these biases...the anthropological codes underline...the differences between the ways of life in force in the culture of the text and in our own and...the significance of acts that, gratuitous to our eyes, are ritualistic in

12. Bal is not opposed to anachronistic readings as such. On the contrary, at certain points and for specific purposes she accepts such a characterization of some of her own readings (see, for example, Bal 1987: 132; 1991a: 239). What does trouble her is an anachronistic reading which passes itself off as 'the true meaning' of the text without sufficient regard for the fact of cultural difference.

context. The result is that these codes are capable of contributing to the critical enterprise *by actively resisting the anachronistic prejudices that pass unnoticed with the help of the ethnocentric code.* (Bal 1988a: 73, emphasis mine)

In addition to helping the interpreter foster this 'critical attitude', anthropology can supply the reader with more specific information that aids in the construction of heuristic reading hypotheses. Bal recognizes that ancient texts are often impossible to read without presupposing some sort of shared framework of meaning (see, for example, Bal 1988a: 59). Faced with this difficulty, and sensitive to the danger of projecting one's own cultural assumptions upon the culture which produced the texts, the interpreter can call upon particular anthropological theories and utilize them as tools for the practice of reading.

In her own readings of biblical texts, Bal appeals to different sorts of anthropological research in exactly this way. For example, she discusses Judges 4 in relation to the anthropology of honor and shame (Bal 1988a: 116-120; cf. 1990c). The most extensive use of anthropology as a source for the construction of specific hypotheses is her argument, especially in *Death and Dissymmetry* (1988b; cf. also 1990a), that the violence which manifests itself in Judges can be related to a shift in the structures of marriage and kinship. By reconsidering the book in the light of an alternative anthropological view of kinship and marriage relations, Bal is able not only to offer an interpretation of the passages in question (which interpretation can then, as can all interpretations, be evaluated for its plausibility by other scholars) but also to highlight the extent to which previous interpretations have in fact rested upon certain views of the social presuppositions of the book of Judges which are less than self-evident.

Narratology, Power, and Representation

Bal also claims that the 'relevance' of her narratological method 'lies in its inherent power to underscore power' (Bal 1988b: 38). Although Bal is less explicit on the meaning and implications of this point than we might wish, certain tentative conclusions can be reached.

First, narrative texts portray relations of power. They represent situations in which power is unequally distributed among the characters. When we interpret a particular text we can consider carefully the power which some characters appear to have over others or wish to gain over others. Such a consideration can apply to groups as well as individuals, so that we must learn to recognize when a certain class of persons (say, women or slaves) does or does not have access to the same power held by other classes (say, men or free persons) in the narrative.

However, it is important not to make hasty or unequivocal judgments about this point, such that all characters are considered either to have or not to have power. There are more possibilities than only these two, as theorists of power have increasingly come to emphasize (see, for example, Foucault 1978; 1980; cf. Fewell and Gunn 1993: 15). To give one example, a character whose powers are limited may nevertheless be represented as exercising a certain amount of power within the constraints that are imposed upon that character. Such a relative exercise of power can contribute to the meaning of a text, even when the existence of the constraints in question is acknowledged.

Bal seems to suggest this point when she resists the notion that the situation of female characters must always be described as either 'good' or 'bad' (Bal 1988b: 34). It is helpful to work instead with a more nuanced view which, on the one hand, does not deny the reality of male dominance (in both the society that produced the biblical texts and in the texts themselves) but which, on the other hand, does not ignore the possibilities for meaningful female action within the circumscribed realm of possibilities. Such a view coheres well with the goals of those anthropologists who recognize the reality and extent of male dominance cross-culturally but who also take into account both the possible variations of such dominance and the strategies that women use to maximize their influence and autonomy within the limits imposed upon them.[13]

However, when Bal speaks about 'the language of power' (1988b: 32), she is not only talking about an analysis of the power relations which appear to exist in the world represented by a narrative. She seems to be saying, in addition, that narrative discourse, as a representation, is itself constituted through certain power relations inasmuch as the power to speak about the world, to show one's vision of the world, and to act upon and in response to the world is granted to some rather than others. Bal's narratological theory implies that narrative discourse always entails a selection on the part of its author. This selection results in a particular configuration of subjects and objects, since it involves a choice not only among different kinds of actions carried out by different kinds of actors but also among the points of view from which such actions and actors

---

13. An excellent overview of these issues can be found in Moore 1988.

can be seen. When these selections and choices are made, certain options are ruled out, and we can therefore think of the narrative texts that result as, themselves, produced by and enacting relations of power.

This aspect of Bal's narratology also coheres quite well with some of the most recent developments in anthropology (cf. Clifford and Marcus [eds.] 1986; Clifford 1988; Fabian 1983; Rosaldo 1989). Certain anthropologists, concerned as they are with the representation of otherness (in their case, the description of other cultures), are now struggling with the question of the power relations inscribed within ethnographic representation. Attempting to represent the views of others, anthropologists speak in a voice which is their own and necessarily make choices about language and focalization, choices that result in a structure which can scarcely be identical to the self-representations of the members of the cultures in question. Bal herself recognizes that the issues at stake in these anthropological discussions are related to, if not identical with, the conceptualization of power and narrative discourse with which she has tried to come to terms in developing her narratology (cf., for example, Bal 1990b; 1993).

Both sorts of power relations can be considered during the course of a narrative analysis. On the one hand, we can ask about the distribution of power among the characters who inhabit the world of the narrative. On the other hand, we can ask about the power which is exercised at the moment of the narrative's construction, distributing the position of acting subject, focalizing subject or speaking subject to some characters rather than others, and thereby manipulating our perception of the events and characters by controlling both that which we see and that which we can only imagine.

These questions bring Bal's narratological method into the realm of ideological analysis. In spite of the difficulties involved in defining the term 'ideology' (cf. Eagleton 1991), a number of biblical scholars have argued for the relevance of an 'ideological criticism' in biblical studies, since it helps to underscore the fact that texts, including biblical texts, 'simultaneously preserve and promote certain views about power relations and social identity' (Weems 1992: 26).[14] One way in which this happens is by representing social relations in specific ways and from specific points of view. The representation of social relationships helps to

14. *Semeia* 59 is devoted entirely to the 'Ideological Criticism of Biblical Texts'. Many of the essays in this volume have been influenced by the work of Fredric Jameson (see especially Jameson 1981), which has also had an influence upon Bal.

'naturalize' these relationships (cf. Belsey 1980). Such a representation offers positions with which readers are asked to identity and from which readers are asked to consider the world. If, as Maaike Meijer states, 'what we experience as reality is formed through the represented' with which we come in contact, then we need to 'look more closely at *how* a text works', and to consider 'the ways in which texts produce subject- and object-positions, and how these positions are distributed' and upon what bases (Meijer 1993: 368-69). Bal's narratological method offers one tool for such a project, though this tool must, as she recognizes, be supplemented by other tools, such as anthropology, that analyze the social and cultural formations in relation to which structures of representation are generated.

Chapter 4

TEXTUAL ANALYSES

Introduction

In the pages that follow, six texts are examined in the light of the preceding methodological discussions. Each text, found within the body of literature widely referred to as the 'Deuteronomistic History', has been selected because it presents material which is related to or has been perceived as being related to sexual activity. At a certain point in all but one of these narratives,[1] a form of sexual contact figures in the plot. At these same points, the postulation of an implicit network of assumptions about sexual activity seems to be necessary for a plausible reading. Our task includes a determination of, on the one hand, the contribution of the sexual act to the plot and, on the other, the degree to which these texts presuppose or interact with the cultural assumptions about sexual activity and its symbolic significance outlined above.

Thus, literary and socio-cultural concerns are both emphasized, and necessarily so. Narratology and anthropology are utilized as tools, useful for the construction of an interpretation which can account for the complicated semiotic process involved in reading biblical narratives. The argument of this chapter is a cumulative one. While the texts discussed here are in many ways quite diverse, similarities between the otherwise heterogeneous texts will be noted. The similarities have to do not only with the appearance of sexual elements per se, but also with particular uses of sexual rhetoric and with structural relations in each text that shed light on the entire group of texts. Thus, the argument does not rest on the reading of any one text in isolation from the others, and the next

1. As I explain in detail below, the narrative of the dispute between Adonijah and Solomon in 1 Kgs 2, which does not actually recount an instance of sexual contact, is often interpreted in relation to two of the other stories discussed here which do recount instances of sexual contact. This history of interpretation justifies the inclusion of a discussion of 1 Kgs 2.

chapter will summarize continuities brought out by the readings.

This project is not tied to any particular source analysis or theory of production of the Deuteronomistic History, and I offer neither a critique nor a defense of such theories.[2] My purpose is to examine certain views on sexual practice and consider their relation to particular texts. While the final chapter reflects briefly on the relation between these stories and theories about the Deuteronomistic History, the idea of a 'Deuteronomistic History' functions largely to define the scope of the project: narratives within the Former Prophets will be examined and not, say, narratives from Genesis. Whether or not the similarities that exist among the narratives under consideration, as regards the representation of sexual activity, are any greater than those which might exist between these same stories and other biblical texts not examined here will have to be decided on the basis of further analysis. One cannot simply presuppose a unified approach to sexual activity in the biblical books. There may not be *a* 'biblical view' of sexual activity, or even a single view of sexual activity within the conventional bounds of the Deuteronomistic History. However, I argue that there are certain structural and ideological similarities which recur in the narratives examined here. A narratological and anthropological analysis of these texts can appreciate the differences among them while nevertheless seeing each story as a manifestation of a particular complex of ideological assumptions about sexual practice.

Judges 19

The story recounted in Judges 19 falls within the enigmatic final five chapters (17–21) of the book of Judges. This entire section is generally considered an 'appendix' (Soggin 1981: 261; Talmon 1986: 39; Brettler 1989: 408) or 'epilogue' (Mayes 1983: 61), added at a late stage of the book's compositional history. The parts of these chapters are knitted together with the observation 'In those days there was not a king in Israel', twice in this form (18.1; 19.1) and twice with the additional observation that 'each man did what was right in his eyes' (17.6; 21.25).

2. Those interested in the debate can consult the standard sources, such as Noth 1991; Cross 1973; Nelson 1981; Friedman 1981; Smend 1971; Dietrich 1972; Veijola 1975; 1977; Mayes 1983; Van Seters 1983; Halpern 1988. One indication of the influence of this debate is the fact that even scholars who take a literary approach to the 'Deuteronomistic History' often justify their methods over against the works just cited. Cf., for instance, Polzin 1989: 1-17; Mullen 1993: 3-9.

This recurring editorial comment contextualizes the two stories within the disorder and social chaos that, it is implied, characterized the period prior to the introduction of monarchy (see Soggin 1989: 203; 1981: 265).[3] The overall portrait of Israel found in these chapters seems, therefore, to be focalized negatively.

As a result of the events narrated in ch. 19, all of the tribes of Israel unite against the tribe of Benjamin in what appears to be an instance of 'holy war' directed against one of Israel's constituent parts. This aspect of the tale has occupied the minds of historical critics, who employ it in their attempt to reach conclusions about the political and religious structures of premonarchic Israel.[4]

Certain elements of ch. 19 are strikingly similar to the more familiar story of Lot and Sodom, found in Genesis 19. Thus, scholars have investigated the relationship between the two stories, sometimes arguing for the priority of one text over the other (for example, Soggin 1981: 288; Brettler 1989: 411; Niditch 1982: 375-78; Lasine 1984) and sometimes arguing for the undecidability (for example, Culley 1976) of what is nevertheless assumed by the scholars to be a relevant question, namely, 'Which of the stories is based upon the other?' However, discussions carried out within the framework of newer literary approaches tend to place less emphasis on questions of priority and dependence. The two stories can, for example, be seen as 'type-scenes' in the sense discussed by Alter: their effect depends upon 'the manipulation of a fixed constellation of predetermined motifs' (Alter 1981: 51) in a predominantly oral/aural culture. Alternatively, some readers prefer to speak of the relationship between the two stories in terms of the literary-critical concept of 'intertextuality' (for example Penchansky 1992).

Although the events of chs. 19–21 are frequently regarded as among the most horrible in the Hebrew Bible, constituting, in the words of one reader, 'a world of unrelenting terror' (Trible 1984: 65), the text itself contains few evaluative statements from the narrator. Explicit judgments about who is considered to have acted appropriately or inappropriately, and upon what bases, are infrequent. We are not even told specifically who is responsible for the actual killing of the young woman, the men

---

3.   For a different view, cf. Talmon 1986: 39-52.

4.   Noth, for example, used the story to discuss the functioning of the premonarchic 'amphictyony' in his well-known hypothesis about the political and religious organization of early Israel (Noth 1960: 105; see also Noth 1930: 162ff.; Mayes 1974).

who rape her or the man who cuts her into twelve pieces.

The story begins with a Levite who resides in the hill-country of Ephraim. This Levite acquires a 'concubine' (פילגש) from Bethlehem. Bal (1988b) argues that the term פילגש refers to a wife who lives with her father. However, as Exum (1993: 177) points out, this argument does not account adequately for other uses of the term. 2 Sam. 16.20-22, discussed below, does not fit Bal's thesis. Thus, the conventional translation 'concubine' is retained here in spite of the fact that, as Bal correctly points out, the exact nature of the role signified by פילגש (and its difference from אשה, 'wife') is difficult to specify.

After some time, the woman leaves the Levite and returns to her father's house in Bethlehem. The verb used to describe the woman's action toward the Levite in the Masoretic Text is זנה (ותזנה עליו פילגשו) and her action has sometimes been assigned a sexual content based upon this verb. The KJV, for example, rendered the verb 'played the whore'. This translation interprets the woman's action as an act of sexual unfaithfulness toward the Levite. On the basis of this word, it might seem that the sexual elements of the story begin at this early point in the chapter.

This interpretation is curious, however, as several scholars (for instance, Boling 1975: 273; Exum 1993: 178) point out. The woman leaves the Levite not to live with another man in either a marital or sexual sense, as one might expect were sexual fidelity the issue, but rather to return to her father's house. Moreover, sexual activity on her part seems unrelated to the story which follows: there is no clear motivation for its appearance. Exum does suggest that one function of the entire story, including the violent treatment of the woman, is to demonstrate the consequences of female sexual infidelity. However, this suggestion cannot account for the violent intentions of the men of Gibeah, who first threaten the Levite rather than the woman.

Certain features of the story are difficult to interpret if sexual infidelity on the woman's part is understood here. For example, the Levite's desire to set out after the woman 'to speak to her heart' (לדבר על לבה, 19.3) leads some commentators (for instance, Soggin 1981: 284; Boling 1975: 274) to suggest that it is the woman rather than the Levite who has been offended. Moreover, there is no hint that the Levite considers divorcing the woman or bringing some sort of charge of adultery against her. Nor does he seek her execution as other biblical texts (such as the story of Judah and Tamar in Gen. 38) might lead us to expect in a case of female sexual infidelity.

Thus, scholars have not universally accepted the notion that we are to understand the woman to have committed some sort of sexual misconduct. Consequently, alternative readings outside the Masoretic tradition have been noted. The Septuagint text of Codex Alexandrinus is frequently cited in this regard, for it tells us that the woman 'became angry' with the Levite and, on the basis of this anger, decided to leave him. This reading has been followed by several modern translations (for instance, RSV, NRSV, NEB) and modern commentators (for instance, Boling 1975: 273; Soggin 1981: 284). If the text of Alexandrinus is adopted here instead of the Masoretic Text, then sexual misconduct on the woman's part does not seem to be a part of the story.

However, explanations of the difference in meaning between Codex Alexandrinus and the Masoretic use of the verb זנה vary. Soggin points to an Akkadian root *zenu*, also mentioned in the critical apparatus to *BHS* at this verse, in order to argue that the verb זנה can sometimes be translated 'quarrelled' (Soggin 1981: 284; cf. Barr 1987: 286) and that Alexandrinus understood it in this sense. Boling lists as possible Hebrew precursors of Alexandrinus זעף ('be out of humor, vexed, enraged'), זעם ('be indignant'), and זנח ('reject, spurn'). He acknowledges that the last possibility could be most easily argued on the basis of the confusion between ה and ח. Nevertheless, he leans toward זעף which does occur elsewhere with the preposition על in a context where, as here, the 'heart' of the angry person is mentioned (ועל יהוה יזעף לבו, 'and against YHWH his heart is vexed', Prov. 19.3b).

Boling goes on to suggest that the Masoretic Text is 'interpretive' in the second verse of Judges 19: 'As Israelite law did not allow for divorce by the wife, she became an adulteress by walking out on him' (1975: 274). This argument rests upon the recognition that it would be quite unusual for a woman to leave her husband in this manner. Narratologically, the woman is an acting subject here in a way that is quite extraordinary within the Hebrew Bible. Thus, Boling argues that the unusual actions taken by the woman in leaving her husband may have motivated a later interpretation of her unconventional activity *as* sexual infidelity or *as analogous to* sexual activity, an interpretation reflected in the appearance of the Hebrew verb זנה in the Masoretic Text.

Even if we admit uncertainty on the question of whether the Masoretic Text or Codex Alexandrinus preserves the 'better' text, Boling's thesis raises the question of the possible evaluation of the woman's conduct by an ancient audience, particularly in the light of the anthropological discussions reviewed above. A portion of that literature, it will be recalled, suggests that the actions taken by or toward a woman are often evaluated *in terms of their impact upon the prestige of the man or men with whom the woman is associated.* If Judges 19 emerged out of a cultural matrix in which gender roles were sharply distinguished and the honor of the husband was partially contingent upon the actions of the women of his household, then this particular woman's act might put the Levite's honor in doubt from the beginning of the story. Moreover, this is actually true whether the woman simply left her husband (following Alexandrinus) or committed adultery against him (following the Masoretic Text), although the situation would no doubt be more severe in the latter case. Sexual infidelity and a more general initiative on the part of the woman to remove herself from her husband's power may be sufficiently close, in terms of their impact upon the evaluation of the male subject, to fall within the same realm of meaning (cf. Exum 1993: 178-80; Fewell and Gunn 1993: 133).

Therefore, this Levite's ability to function in the socially defined role of 'husband' might already be compromised by his concubine's unconventional step, whether this step is construed as illicit sexual activity or an abandonment of her husband. In either case, the man fails to maintain the order of his household in a socially approved manner. Thus, one function of the opening scene may be precisely to question the Levite's ability to embody socially appropriate norms, norms that are related to concepts of gender. Such a questioning of the Levite's status as a gendered subject then sets the stage for a further attack upon his culturally defined masculinity in the story that follows, an attack via the threat of homosexual rape. Indeed, the entire story is placed immediately after a story in which another Levite acts in an unconventional and, from the perspective of the Deuteronomistic History, disapproved manner. The context, then, may lead a reader to wonder from the beginning if this second Levite will also act in socially disapproved ways.

The woman's actions thus function in the narrative in part to characterize the Levite rather than simply the woman herself. This interpretation coheres well with the narratological fact that the woman's active subject position at the beginning of the story contrasts strongly with the positions that she occupies (or rather, fails to occupy) in the remainder of the chapter. We are told nothing more about her actions, thoughts, or speech until the point at which, having been turned over to the men of Gibeah and raped, she returns to the house from which she has been cast. This lack of subject positioning can indicate that the narrative is generally uninterested in the woman herself, and so it supports the argument that her initial actions are recounted in part to cast doubt upon the Levite's character.

The Levite goes after the woman to convince her to return to him. Arriving in Bethlehem, he is greeted enthusiastically by the woman's father. A hospitality scene follows in which the father repeatedly convinces the Levite to delay his departure to Ephraim. Several evenings later, the Levite finally leaves for home, accompanied by the young woman and a male servant. We are not told whether the woman agrees to this arrangement or whether the matter is decided for her; only the male characters speak. This narratological fact might indicate that the woman's own opinion on the matter was not considered to be particularly relevant by the narrator or the characters (cf. Trible 1984: 69). There is no indication in the text that the woman has changed her mind (it was she who left him), and while the narrator does state that the Levite wished to speak to the woman's heart, no conversation between them is ever reported.

On the return journey, the Levite declines to spend the night in Jebus (Jerusalem) and decides to travel on to Gibeah, a city associated with the Benjaminites, rather than spend the night in a non-Israelite city. Upon arrival in Gibeah, the travelers have some difficulty obtaining a place to stay. Eventually, an elderly resident of the town, himself an Ephraimite, offers them hospitality for the night. That a resident alien rather than a native of Gibeah welcomes the travelers is of course parallel to the story of Lot and Sodom (Gen. 19), but in this case the failure of the citizens of Gibeah to offer hospitality seems to be emphasized. Whereas Lot hurries to offer hospitality in Genesis 19, here the travelers wait in the square for some time. Taken together with the events that follow, the failure of the people of Gibeah to offer hospitality to the travelers is a means of characterizing the city of Gibeah negatively.

While the travelers are eating and drinking, a number of the men of the city—described by the narrator as 'worthless fellows' (אנשׁי בני־בליעל)—surround the house and demand that the Levite be brought out so that 'we might know him' (נדענו). 'Knowledge' is apparently used here, as in a number of other instances in biblical narrative (for example, Gen. 4.1, 17, 25), to signify sexual contact. Boswell (1980: 92-98) questions this interpretation, arguing that the men of Gibeah, as well as the men of Sodom in Genesis 19, simply want to find out the identity of ('know') the strangers. However, Boswell's argument is weakened in Judg. 19.25 where the narrator specifies that, after the woman is thrown outside, the men of Gibeah 'knew her and mistreated her' (וידעו אותה ויתעללו בה) all night. This notation comes shortly after the host's suggestion, discussed below, that the men of Gibeah 'abuse' his daughter and the concubine (וענו אותם, 19.24), using a verbal root (ענה) that is used elsewhere in biblical narrative (for instance, 2 Sam. 13.12, 14, 22, 32) to refer to forced sexual intercourse (cf. Keefe 1993: 81). If the eventual treatment of the woman is taken into account, then it appears that the men of Gibeah demand sexual access to the Levite, just as the men of Sodom demand sexual access to Lot's visitors in Genesis 19.

The message of the men of Gibeah therefore has a sexual content. A collective male subject (the worthless fellows of Gibeah) demands sexual contact with a male object (the Levite). For comparative purposes, this message can be represented graphically as follows:

men of Gibeah >> Levite

in which the double arrow represents both a desire for sexual access and the subject–object relation.

The narrated reactions of both host and Levite indicate that the desire for homosexual access is viewed negatively. On the other hand, the negative reaction has not always invited further analysis. Scholars have only infrequently considered that the ideological bases for the negative evaluation in the text might be different from those undergirding the negative evaluation which such actions might receive in the social context of the scholars themselves. In order to analyze the semiotics of this text, however, one must inquire into the range of meanings which might be associated with homosexual contact, and more specifically with the particular form homosexual contact takes here: a threat of rape, which implies both violence against and power over the object of the rape.

Modern beliefs about 'sexual orientation' as a means of classifying types of human subjects may be misleading when applied to ancient texts which do not presuppose such a system of classification (see Foucault 1978; 1985; Weeks 1985; Halperin 1990; but cf. Richlin 1993). However, some consideration of anthropological discussions may be more helpful here. Several anthropologists (see for instance Gilmore [ed.] 1987; Brandes 1981) have indicated that in those cultures manifesting the dynamics of honor and shame, male homosexuality is often viewed with particular distaste. This distaste is associated with the rigid differentiation between male and female gender roles, but also with the hierarchical nature of this differentiation. Masculinity is considered by many of the men of these cultures to be not only different from femininity, but also superior to it. Hence, it is nearly always considered an insult to say that a man is acting like a woman.

Within this network of meaning, male homosexuality comes to assume a particular significance. Of the two men associated with any particular homosexual act, one of the men assumes a role that is, culturally speaking, allotted to the female alone. Stated another way, one male assumes the role *of sexual object* rather than that of sexual subject, a role which is assumed to be 'normal' for the female but not for the male (cf. Lancaster 1988; 1992: 235-78). The male who allows himself to be (or is unable to prevent himself from being) *acted upon* sexually shows himself to be the object of another man; he therefore becomes 'feminized'. This man is without honor because he is, so to speak, no longer considered a man. The negative attitude toward homosexuality can thus be seen within this ideological complex as a function of gender differentiation and hierarchy.

Consequently, male homosexual contact comes to serve metaphorically for other sorts of unequal male–male power relations. Sexual penetration signifies social submission. Stanley Brandes gives an example of such a metaphorical function of male homosexuality when he calls attention to the phrase 'lowering our trousers', used by men as a metaphor for being forced into a situation in which they were put under the power or at the mercy of other males (Brandes 1981: 232-234; cf. Delaney 1991: 50). The metaphor is effective precisely because sexual submission signifies, within this network of meaning, a 'feminine' role and, hence, the demasculinization of the man forced to take this role. By taking on the 'female' position, the man assumes a position characterized generally, in these cultures, by lower status and power.

The link between sexual penetration and social submission appears not only in ethnographic sources but in the ancient world as well, even in cultures such as ancient Greece which are sometimes characterized in terms of their 'acceptance' of male homosexuality. Several recent studies have argued that the terms of this 'acceptance' are actually constituted by a clear recognition of the unequal social roles of the two partners involved. Certain types of homosexual relationships were indeed an accepted part of many Greco-Roman societies. However, the penetration of an adult male citizen in these same cultures usually implies, in fact, a negative perspective on the man who allows himself to be penetrated. The act places him in a position reserved for women, boys, and slaves: appropriate objects of pleasure for the adult male subject of sexual practice (cf. Dover 1989; Winkler 1990: 45-70; Halperin 1990: 15-71; Keuls 1985: 274-99; Foucault 1985: 187-225).

Thus, if we want to characterize the difference between attitudes toward homosexuality found in ancient Greek and Roman societies, on the one hand, and attitudes found in a number of traditional but relatively recent societies studied by anthropologists, on the other hand, it may not be entirely helpful to refer to an 'acceptance' of homosexuality by the former over against a 'rejection' of homosexuality by many of the latter. In both cases, male homosexuality takes on significance in terms of unequal social positions and power relations. One partner is placed within a position 'properly' shared by individuals of a lower social status. The real difference is that, whereas males in both groups of societies consider male citizens to be appropriate sexual subjects, and all women to be appropriate sexual objects (at least for the male citizens), the ancient Greeks seem to have collocated boys and slaves (of whatever gender) together with women in the latter category. In both cases, however, a distinction between socially approved subject and object positions determines the dominant attitude toward male homosexuality.

If we attempt to frame the biblical texts in terms of this discussion, we can argue that the attitude found there seems congruent with certain recurring beliefs about the significance of male homosexuality, while falling closer to the end of a spectrum of variations which it shares with most of the ethnographic cases. Like Brandes's informants, the authors of the biblical traditions may have associated male homosexuality with social submission (and hence humiliation), but assigned the position of proper 'sexual object' in terms of which the humiliated male was defined primarily to women alone rather than to boys and slaves as well. Men who are sexual objects in relation to other men are symbolically emasculated; they are associated with women, who as a group are in official discourse assumed to be of lower social status than men.

This interpretation is not necessarily contradicted by the Levitical laws, which prescribe death for both the active and the passive partners of male homosexual intercourse. The Hebrew Bible has few references to homosexuality of any sort. The only clear references, apart from Judges 19 and its parallel in Genesis 19, are found in Lev. 18.22 and

20.13.[5] Both Levitical texts refer to specifically male homosexual inter-course. Both texts also signify male homosexual contact by way of a contrast with heterosexual intercourse. The male addressees of the legal formulations are forbidden to lie with men in the manner in which, it is said, one lies with women.

This way of referring to male homosexual intercourse in terms of male/female sexual roles signals the importance of gender role definition in the stance taken by the biblical text toward male homosexual contact. The activity proscribed is one in which a male is understood to act toward another male in the manner in which a male acts, conventionally, toward a woman. Stated in terms of the subject–object distinction: according to the Levitical laws, a male subject should not treat another male as sexual object. The latter position is allotted to the woman alone. Similarly, a male should not take this object-position upon himself. Male homosexual contact is forbidden because it confuses categories: a male, properly the sexual subject in relation to a female sexual object, is placed in the role of sexual object where he does not belong. This confusion is abominable to the authors of the Levitical codes, who go to great lengths to map out the distinctions and categories by which the world ought to be ordered and to condemn any activity or object which disrupts this system (cf. Douglas 1966; Olyan 1994; Gottwald 1985: 473-78).

Female homosexual contact, however, is not mentioned at all in the Hebrew Bible.[6] The possibility of a female sexual subject acting in rela-tion to a female sexual object may have simply been meaningless within the symbolic and ideological framework which shapes these texts. Within this worldview, women seem to have been, by definition, normatively con-fined to the status of sexual object (cf. Fewell and Gunn 1993: 107-108).

A similar concern about the relationship among gender roles, subject/object positions in sexual practice, and male homosexual contact probably

5.   For an excellent historical-critical discussion of these texts, see Olyan 1994.

6.   As James Barr pointed out to me after reading an earlier version of this chapter, the silence of the Hebrew Bible about female homoeroticism raises the question, which requires further analysis, of why the apostle Paul, for example, in Rom. 1, does speak against such activity. For an excellent analysis of this question which makes use of Mary Douglas's purity theories, see Brooten 1985. Brooten, too, argues that gender roles are at stake in the negative evaluation of homosexuality, but shows that the question of proper *female* sexual roles has apparently also been problematized in Jewish literature by the time of Paul. Cf. also Pseudo-Phocylides 192 where, after a condemnation of male homosexuality, women are forbidden to 'imitate the sexual role of men' (Van Der Horst 1985: 581).

underlies the use of male homosexual rape in Judges 19 as a culturally determined way of characterizing negatively the intentions of the men of Gibeah. Within a culture marked by rigid gender differentiation and hierarchy, a man who assumes the role allotted by convention to a woman is moving, socially, *downward*. If this role is forced upon him by another male, as is the case in homosexual rape, then the effect is both a challenge to his masculinity and a challenge to his honor. The subject of the rape, the man who does the forcing, is thereby making a statement about the inability of the male object to emulate a certain socially inscribed model of masculinity. This is also a statement about relative power relations, since by definition men are considered to have power over women (just as, in the Greek case, men are considered to have power over women, boys, and slaves).[7] Thus, we can say that in our initial graphic representation:

men of Gibeah (male) >> Levite (male)

the relation in question is not simply one of desire. It is also one of power (the men of Gibeah wish to express their power over the Levite) and honor (the men of Gibeah wish to bring dishonor and shame upon the Levite).

The insult constituted by this challenge seems to be compounded within the narrative discourse by the fact that the message is conveyed not directly to the Levite, but rather to the host. The Levite is not only an object of the intended actions of the men of Gibeah, he is also an object of speech. The men of Gibeah do not speak *to* him, even by command, but rather speak *about* him to the host, who is thus given control over the disposal of the Levite's sexuality—exactly as men are generally given sovereignty over sexual access to women.

Here, however, the demand conflicts with the norms of hospitality. Hospitality seems to have been accorded a great deal of value in ancient Israel (cf. Matthews 1992; Matthews and Benjamin [eds.] 1993: 82-95; Wright 1989) and in other parts of the ancient world (Finley 1978: 124-26). Many social scientists have pointed out that hospitality can be quite

---

7.   This set of symbolic meanings may also account for other ancient Near Eastern references to homosexuality. A particularly significant Egyptian case is the story of Horus and Seth, in which Seth makes of Horus a sexual object and then brags in court about having 'done a man's deed to him' (Lichtheim 1976: 220). A thorough comparative study of ancient Near Eastern references to homosexuality is long overdue. One compilation of the evidence by a non-specialist can be found in Greenberg 1988: 124-41.

significant for the evaluation of personal and familial honor (see Pitt-Rivers 1977: 94-112; Nieuwenhuijze 1971: 286-87; Herzfeld 1987). A number of biblical scholars have linked the interpretation of this particular story to a transgression of hospitality rituals (see for instance Parker 1991; Penchansky 1992; Matthews 1992). The obligation of host 'to protect his guest or the honour of his guest' (Pitt-Rivers 1977: 110) supplies a specific motivation for the Ephraimite host to decline to oblige the men of Gibeah. He urges them not to 'act wickedly' (אל־תרעו נא) by doing 'this disgraceful thing' (אל־תעשׂו את־הנבלה הזאת). The host offers instead his own daughter and the concubine and suggests that the men 'afflict them (וענו אותם) and do whatever you want to them; but against this man do not do this disgraceful thing' (19.24). The term 'disgraceful thing' (נבלה) will also be used in 2 Samuel 13 where, once again, it is associated with rape.

The response of the old man takes the form of a negotiation. He attempts to deter the men of Gibeah by offering two alternative sexual objects: his own daughter and the Levite's companion. In other words, he attempts to replace a male object with two female objects: to prevent the rape of one man, the host offers the rape of two women. This offer is comparable to Genesis 19, where Lot offers his daughters as sexual objects in place of the male visitors. Clearly the alternative is considered preferable in both texts, even by the daughter's own father: better to hand over my daughter, who is at any rate a *proper sexual object*, than my male guest(s), who is properly a *sexual subject* and, moreover, the recipient of hospitality. Thus, on the one hand, by referring in such a negative manner ('this disgraceful thing') to the proposed deed of the men of Gibeah, the host *focalizes* it for them: it is evaluated negatively. But on the other hand, by offering the two women as objects of rape, the host focalizes that act as well: however reprehensible the act might be in isolation, it is considered a more acceptable alternative.

The host thus introduces the two women into what has been, up to now, an exclusively male transaction. The sender of the message (men of Gibeah) is male, the receiver of the message (host) is male, and the object of the message (Levite) is male. The host's attempt to replace the demand of the men of Gibeah with an alternative can be represented as follows:

men of Gibeah (male) >> two women (female)

Since the women are, from the perspective of the subject of focalization, already below the male Levite on the scale of social differentiation, the degree of offense is considered less severe. The women have, so to speak, less distance to fall by being brought under the power of the men of the city. This is not to say that the rape of the woman was not in itself offensive. Subsequent events indicate that it was considered quite offensive, although we should be careful to raise the question of *who* was actually considered the offended party (the woman or the Levite). However, the point remains that the host, as well as Lot (the one 'righteous man' in the city of Sodom), found women to be more acceptable objects of rape than men, and this attitude is never condemned by the text.

The men of Gibeah reject the bargain, however. The Levite then grabs the concubine and throws her out to the crowd. Clearly, he agrees with the host that the rape of the women (or, at the very least, of one of the women) is preferable to his own rape. Although the men outside the house rejected the offer of the host's daughter and the concubine, they accept the offer of the concubine alone. They abuse her all night, in spite of their initial refusal to accept two women for one man. Only a few commentators (see, for instance, Exum 1993: 183; Bal 1988b: 120) have asked for an explanation of this sudden willingness to accept part of an offer which has just been rejected.

A specific interpretation of this fact can be offered in light of the preceding discussion. It must be recalled that the men of Gibeah threaten the Levite, but state no hostile intentions toward the host. It must also be recalled, from the anthropological material, that not only a woman's conduct but also the conduct taken toward her may reflect upon the honor of the male(s) responsible for her. A sexual misconduct committed against a woman is, therefore, an attack upon the man under whose authority she falls. Thus, although the men of Gibeah did not dishonor the Levite directly by raping him *as if he were a woman*, they nevertheless challenge his honor in another way: *through his woman*.

For this reason the offer of the daughter and the concubine is rebuffed, while the offer of the concubine alone is successful. The men of Gibeah are not interested in attacking the host; rather, they want his guest. Although the actions of the men of the city would, by thwarting his act of hospitality, certainly rob the host of an opportunity to increase his honor, the story turns upon the fact that the men wish to humiliate the Levite, not the host who dwells among them. Thus, they do not want the host's daughter, whose rape would impact only the honor of the host, but they accept the woman associated with the Levite. The men of Gibeah still manage to inflict dishonor upon the Levite, and to do so in a sexual manner. Hence, we can restate our representation of the situation as follows:

men of Gibeah >> concubine >> Levite

The men of Gibeah attack the Levite, and they do so in a sexual manner: *by way of* the concubine. At the very least, the rape of the woman reflects negatively upon the honor of the Levite. The men of Gibeah convey the message to the Levite that their power will prevail over his. The concubine serves as the 'conduit of a relationship', in Rubin's terminology, a relationship of power between the men of Gibeah and the Levite.

Yet it seems to be the Levite himself who throws his concubine to the men of the city. Thus, one might be inclined to ask why he would perform an action which ultimately reflects dishonor upon himself. Within the logic of the narrative, however, the Levite may have no positive choice: it is either the rape of the concubine or his own rape, and though the choice he makes may seem reprehensible from our viewpoint, there is little evidence in this text or in Genesis 19 that might indicate anything but approval for the substitution per se. The rape of the concubine is seen as the lesser evil of two alternatives available to the Levite. Indeed, we have to consider the possibility that an ancient, and perhaps largely male, audience (more influenced by notions of gender-based honor than, say, Anglo-American concepts of 'chivalry' or ideas about gender equity) would have seen the Levite's actions in this manner.

The Levite is offended by the events that take place. Otherwise, he has little motivation for bringing about the retaliation of Israel against the tribe of Benjamin, which sides with the city of Gibeah. On the basis of the discussion above, however, we can suggest that the Levite retaliates because the actions of the men of Gibeah are interpreted by the Levite (as indeed they are intended to be interpreted) at least in part as actions taken against him and his honor. The man has turned the concubine over to the crowd, but only because he recognizes the point which they have communicated: they are more powerful than he, and one way or the other he will participate in the fulfillment of their desire.

There is, on the other hand, little evidence that the woman's welfare in itself is a major consideration in the Levite's retaliation. Several commentators (see for example Lasine 1984: 44-45; Trible 1984: 79) have noticed the lack of concern for the woman by the Levite: he never speaks to her during the entire transaction, apparently plans to leave without her in the morning, and simply orders her to get up when he finds her upon the doorstep. It would seem that it is not her welfare which motivates his call for retaliation, but rather the damage that he believes has been done to his honor. This same masculine honor, which reflects not only upon the individual but also upon the social group of which he is a part (cf. Pitt-Rivers 1977), requires a riposte from Israel as a whole. Israel's response produces the spiral of death and kidnapping outlined in chs. 20 and 21.

One other curious feature of this story may be illuminated by the symbolic assumptions outlined above. Scholars have long disagreed about the significance of the Levite's words to the assembly at Mizpah in ch. 20. In 20.5, the Levite recounts the events that have taken place in words which are sometimes taken as an intentional misconstrual of the situation. He tells Israel that the men of Gibeah intended to kill him, and that they abused his concubine until she died. He does not mention either their intention to rape him or his own role in throwing the woman to the crowd. Lasine concludes from the Levite's testimony that the Levite is purposely portrayed as 'an irresponsible liar' (Lasine 1984: 48).

However, the Levite's words may in fact express a symbolic confusion which is a crucial part of the ideology of the text. Since the rape of the woman was indeed followed by her death, it is not unreasonable to assume that the rape of the Levite might also have preceded his death. Thus, the Levite may simply be saying that the men of Gibeah initially planned to treat him as they did treat the woman. The interchangeability of the Levite and the woman, and hence of male and female, is precisely what the men of Gibeah wish to communicate to the Levite, and precisely what the Levite communicates to the assembly at Mizpah in turn. Moreover, while we might wish to believe that the men of Israel would have been less eager to retaliate had they been aware that the Levite himself had cast the woman to the crowd in order to prevent his own rape (so Lasine 1984: 49), careful consideration of the words of the host, of the words of Lot in Genesis 19, and of the symbolic assumptions underlying the biblical texts may lead instead to the conclusion that, to the contrary, most of the Israelites would have responded to such a situation in precisely the same way.

For purposes of comparison with the texts that will be analyzed below, it may be helpful to restate in summary what, I am arguing, has happened here. In the first place, a collective male subject challenges the honor of another male. In this case, the nature of the challenge is explicitly sexual.

men of Gibeah >> Levite
male >> male

The relation here is entirely one between men. The challenge to the Levite's honor and power is, however, displaced onto his concubine. Instead of raping the Levite, the men rape the woman.

men of Gibeah >> concubine
male >> female

The Levite is nevertheless upset. A motivation behind his desire for retaliation takes on a specific content in the light of the anthropological frame: the men of Gibeah have still managed to affront his honor, via the woman.

men of Gibeah >> concubine >> Levite
male >> female >> male

Stated in terms of the gender of the actors involved, this structural relation,

male >> female >> male

will occur again and again, in various transformations, in the pages that follow. In almost every case that we will examine, a woman is, or is interpreted to be, or is represented as being, the means with which one male challenges the honor and power of another male. The nature of this challenge is, again and again, sexual. Admittedly, we will not again see a case in which a male subject explicitly utilizes the language of homosexual rape to threaten another male. Nevertheless, we will see in the pages that follow that male characters apparently can carry out indirectly, by means of heterosexual contact, a desire which is expressed more directly here by homosexual rape: that of power over, and dishonor of, another man. The lines between homosexual rape and a more general 'homosocial'[8] conflict thus turn out to be somewhat fluid.

---

8.   The term 'homosocial' has gained some currency following the work of Eve Kosofsky Sedgwick, who uses it in an influential study to describe 'social bonds between persons of the same sex' (Sedgwick 1985: 1). While Sedgwick makes little use of anthropological materials, she has underscored the links among certain sorts of homosocial relations, the domination of women by men, and the suppression of male homoeroticism.

2 Samuel 3.6-11

2 Samuel 3 contains portions of the story of Abner, son of Ner, and his role in the struggle between David and the house of Saul. The incidents which take place in ch. 3 occur, as the narrator tells us (3.1), at a point when the fighting for the throne of Israel has been going on for quite some time. The story of Abner as a whole contains a great deal of information about battles, intrigues, and negotiations. We are told of Abner's defection from the house of Saul to the house of David and of his murder by Joab, David's military chief. The story is clearly a tale about the struggle, among men, for power.

In the midst of this struggle, however, in 2 Sam. 3.6-11, there is a report of a conversation between Abner and Ishbaal (see, on this name, McCarter 1984: 85-86), a surviving son of Saul. Ishbaal is presently ruling over a portion of his father's former kingdom, and it is initially part of Abner's goal to extend Ishbaal's power even further. Yet here, Ishbaal and Abner quarrel. The motivation for this quarrel is a sexual encounter.

The report of the quarrel between Abner and Ishbaal is so brief that it might seem to be insignificant. The narrator tells us that Saul had a concubine named Rizpah, the daughter of Aiah. Like many women in the Hebrew Bible, Rizpah is discussed in this particular text entirely in terms of her relations with men. She is named here, and at a later point in the story of David she will play a more significant role (see 2 Sam. 21.8-14). However, Rizpah herself does not appear on the 'narrative stage' in 2 Samuel 3 at all. Rather, it is Ishbaal and Abner who discuss a sexual relationship between Abner and Rizpah.

Indeed, the sexual act which takes place between Abner and Rizpah is not directly represented in the narrative, at least not in the Masoretic Text. Some Septuagint manuscripts do specify that Abner 'took' or 'went in to' her (cf. McCarter 1984: 105-106), but these specifications are probably additions to the original, shorter text. There is thus no recounting of the activity by the narrator, still less a description. It is Ishbaal who first mentions the sexual contact to Abner, asking him in v. 7, 'Why have you gone in to the concubine of my father?' Here, as in a number of other places, 'going in to' (באתה) is a manner of speaking about sexual activity, and Abner never denies that sexual contact of some sort has taken place. It should be noted, however, that Ishbaal never states any interest in Rizpah's well-being. He seems to be concerned primarily with Abner, with the manner in which Abner has acted, and with Rizpah's role as a female member of the house of Saul. Indeed, Rizpah is not even named by Ishbaal, but is instead referred to by way of her relation with Ishbaal's father: 'the concubine of my father' (פילגש אבי). This designation may itself be significant insofar as it reveals, by specifying the link between Rizpah and Ishbaal's household, the motivation for Ishbaal's question.

The initiative for this sexual contact is placed entirely upon Abner. It is Abner who 'goes in to' the woman. He is the subject of the verb באתה, and hence, within the narrative discourse, of the action as well. This manner of speaking about the sexual activity thus leaves the woman, discursively, in the role of object. Narratologically speaking, Rizpah is not a subject in any sense in this chapter. We do not hear her speech, although she is discussed; hence, she is the object rather than the subject of speech. We do not gain any insight into that which she sees, either literally or figuratively; hence, she is the object rather than the subject of focalization. We are not told how she acts, but rather how she is acted upon; hence, she is the object rather than the subject of (sexual) action. Abner acts sexually in relation to Rizpah, and Ishbaal wants to know why Abner has acted in this particular manner. On the level of language and representation, however, Rizpah does nothing at all. Her motives and opinions are neither asked for nor given, and we have no way of determining if this contact was something she wanted or if, like the Levite's concubine, she was simply taken. Within the discourse *about* Rizpah, both that of the characters and that of the narrator, Rizpah as a possible subject is simply ignored, at least in this chapter.

Although the conversation between Ishbaal and Abner does not take up a great ideal of the narrative, it is, narratologically speaking, quite significant. The conversation is a 'functional' event: once the conversation takes place, it decisively affects the subsequent course of the narrative (Bal 1985: 15). Because of this conversation, Abner will seek to make a covenant with David. Thus, the result of the quarrel is a series of distinctly political facts: Ishbaal will lose the support of his most able military leader, and Abner will attempt to rally Benjamin and Israel behind David. These developments on the level of Israel's national politics will be accompanied by developments of a different sort: Joab will kill Abner in retaliation for Abner's earlier murder of Joab's brother, and David will confess his powerlessness before the actions of the 'sons of Zeruiah', Joab and Abishai. However, the power struggles that result from this conversation are, again, represented primarily in terms of male characters. The only female character other than Rizpah who makes a subsequent appearance in this chapter is Michal, but she, too, functions in terms of the negotiations that take place between male characters: she is returned to David as part of the bargain between Abner and David (3.12-16).

Now obviously the confrontation between Abner and Ishbaal is itself the result of the previous sexual event. The confrontation can only take place because the sexual contact has already taken place. The sexual act might therefore seem to be just as important, within the narrative, as the confrontation between Abner and Ishbaal that results from it. Within the logic of the story's events, the sexual contact initiated by Abner produces (and is considered capable of producing) a dramatic set of political, and quite public, circumstances.

However, the 'event' of the sexual act is not recounted at the logical moment at which it must have taken place, that is, prior to the conversation between the two men. Instead, the relations between fabula and story are ordered here in such a way that the sexual event is only told at the moment of the conversation. This way of ordering the events seems to imply that the sexual act itself is only considered important in its relation to the quarrel between Ishbaal and Abner. There seems to be no interest in the sexual act except as it resulted in this conversation and the events that follow. As is true in the case of other biblical narratives as well, sexual activity seems to be of interest primarily because of its results, and not because sexual matters in and of themselves were considered remarkable (cf. Barr 1992: 67).

Ishbaal's question sounds a good deal more like an accusation than a simple expression of curiosity, since it provokes anger on the part of its addressee, Abner. Abner's anger only makes sense if we as readers reason that he interprets Ishbaal's question as some sort of an accusation. In Abner's response to Ishbaal, he asserts that 'you charge me with a misdeed concerning the woman today' (v. 8). Now if *Ishbaal* is accusing Abner of some misdeed then *Ishbaal* is logically being represented as having interpreted Abner's sexual activity. Abner's sexual actions have some sort of meaning for Ishbaal. They take on a semiotic status: they become a sign, for which Ishbaal has supplied some content. But what, exactly, is the misdeed of which Ishbaal believes Abner to be guilty?

In order to formulate an answer to this question, it is important to pause and consider the complex semiotic process involved in reading what appears to be a simple passage. The passage is an excellent example of Bal's point, in her discussions of focalization, that our interpretation of a narrative is often mediated by our understanding of the characters' interpretations, embedded in the narrative, of the words and actions of one another. To make sense of Ishbaal's question, it seems necessary for readers to attribute some sort of suspicion to him. Otherwise, it is difficult, if not impossible, to make sense of Abner's angry reply. In order to interpret Ishbaal's question, then, the reader must be able to *see Abner's actions as Ishbaal sees them*, must, that is, *focalize* the sexual act from Ishbaal's standpoint. However, since the content of Ishbaal's suspicion is nowhere stated, it must be supplied if one wishes to interpret the passage. An ancient author may have relied upon conventional codes of meaning to facilitate this communication process, but it is precisely these codes and conventions about sexual activity, implicit rather than spelled out, which we as modern readers no longer presuppose.

Consequently, academic readers of this text have frequently offered hypotheses about the social and cultural significance of the sexual act involved here in order to interpret the passage. One particular understanding has been dominant, and it is worth considering in some detail, since it will impact the interpretation of other texts below. A number of interpreters have seen the offense of which Abner is being accused as *a bid for the throne of Israel*, the throne, that is to say, which is currently being occupied by Ishbaal. Based on an analogy between this text and a particular interpretation of 2 Sam. 12.8; 16.22 and 1 Kgs 2.13, scholars have reasoned that, in the eyes of Ishbaal, Abner's sexual relations with Rizpah look suspiciously like an attempt to legitimate Abner's own claim to the throne. Scholars who read the passage in this manner generally argue for or presuppose a close link, in the ancient Near East, between the legitimation of kingship and the taking of a previous king's wives and concubines (cf., for example, Tsevat 1958; Ishida 1977: 74; Hertzberg 1964: 257; Levenson 1978: 27; McCarter 1984: 112-13; Schwartz 1991: 52; Hackett 1992: 92-93; Leach 1969: 69). These arguments usually posit the existence of a sort of custom whereby a successor to the throne takes as his own the harem of a previous king. A corollary of the hypothetical custom supplies a specific content for Ishbaal's accusation: if a new king takes for himself the harem of a previous king, then a man who takes the harem of a living king might in effect be claiming the throne for himself. Jon Levenson and Baruch Halpern, for example, refer to the existence of 'a custom apparently well founded in Israel' by which 'through the carnal knowledge of a suzerain's harem a man could lay claim to suzerainty himself' (Levenson and Halpern 1980: 508). In defense of this statement, they offer references to this text and those in 2 Samuel 16 and 1 Kings 2, albeit without a detailed discussion of any of the cases.

Now this 'custom' is never actually stated in the Hebrew Bible. It is a reading hypothesis, used by scholars to frame the texts in question in order to produce an interpretation. Scholars who utilize this frame recognize that implicit assumptions about sexual practice seem to be presupposed here, and that the positing of some such web of assumptions is necessary to interpret the passage. They also recognize that sexual activity is related in some way to male–male political relations. Nevertheless, the precise symbolic relations involved are somewhat unclear. It generally remains vague, in the discourse of the commentators, why sexual relations might have an impact upon political relations.

To be sure, when it is stated very broadly, a proposed link between kingship and sexual contact with the wives or concubines of a previous king seems plausible. In each of the biblical cases used to support this 'well-founded custom', Israel's kingship is in dispute. All of the cases involve wives or concubines associated in some manner with a king, wives or concubines who become objects of the actions of other men. The question which can be raised here, however, is whether biblical scholars have sufficiently explored either the symbolic significance of this phenomenon or the textual evidence adduced to support it. Might an anthropologically informed reading increase our insight into the levels of meaning that can be found here?

There are some features of this text which, taken together, call the conventional interpretation of Abner's sexual relation with Rizpah, which reads it as a sign for 'the legitimation of Abner's claim to kingship', into question. First, it should be pointed out that Abner's supposed intention to claim the throne is never mentioned in the text. Neither Ishbaal nor, in his heated reply, Abner ever state that Abner might actually be planning to obtain the throne. This 'argument from silence' does not rule out the possibility that we are to infer precisely such a motivation for Abner's actions. On the other hand, it is Abner himself who has made Ishbaal king over Israel (2 Sam. 2.9), and there is no indication prior to the argument over Rizpah that Abner's motives for doing so were insincere.

Moreover, there are explicit indications within Abner's angry reply to Ishbaal that he is quite aware that he will never obtain the throne. When

Abner is challenged by Ishbaal he does not decide to claim the throne for himself, as well he might had he actually been interested in doing so. On the contrary, Abner affirms unequivocally that YHWH will give the kingdom of Saul to David and pledges to help YHWH accomplish this goal. It thus seems likely that Abner does not plan to place himself upon the throne, and that his actions with Rizpah are not an attempt to legitimate a claim to the kingship. Even if Ishbaal does interpret Abner's actions in this manner, it seems clear that his interpretation is simply wrong; he has misread the message which he believes Abner to have been sending.

However, is it necessarily the case that Ishbaal interprets Abner's actions as an actual claim to the throne in the first place? In our present text, neither Ishbaal, the narrator, nor any other character ever states the nature of the misdeed of which Abner is thought to have been guilty. We cannot simply assume that Ishbaal believes Abner has been plotting for the throne. Some sort of argument must be put forward when we supply a content for Ishbaal's suspicion, even though it is true that this content is never made explicit and, hence, must remain at the level of conjecture. I suggest that an anthropological reading sheds a rather different light upon this text, once it is read apart from the other texts in question (whose interpretation is itself in doubt, as we will see) and in the context of the cultural assumptions about sexual activity and masculinity which have been discussed above.

We have already seen in the discussions of anthropological materials that a man is, in many cultures, considered to be at least partially responsible for the sexual purity of the women who are part of his household. Part of his own honor, as a man, is a function of maintaining the sexual purity of these women. His honor and esteem depend not only upon their behavior, but also upon his ability to control sexual access to them. Such women include wives, but also sisters, mothers, daughters, and probably (as I have already indicated in the discussion of Judg. 19) 'concubines' as well.

Rizpah, as the concubine of Saul, would undoubtedly have been numbered among the women upon whom Saul's honor was thought to depend. Upon Saul's death, this role would have logically passed to the person who assumed his position. Ishbaal is thus responsible for the sexuality of Rizpah, at least to the extent that he has actually assumed the role previously occupied by his father (which is, of course, precisely what is in dispute in this chapter). This might mean that he could grant himself access, sexually, to Rizpah, but it might also mean, more generally, that he would gain the power to grant access to Rizpah to someone else. In either case, the disposal of Rizpah's sexuality becomes Ishbaal's responsibility.

Now if we read the narrative in 2 Samuel 3 with these anthropological insights in mind, Ishbaal's suspicions about Abner's actions take on a particular set of meanings. By giving himself sexual access to Rizpah, apparently without consulting Ishbaal or considering Ishbaal's wishes, Abner can be interpreted as having potentially challenged both the honor and the power of Ishbaal. Abner's actions can be taken, and apparently were taken by Ishbaal, as an insult: Ishbaal is not 'good at being a man', since he cannot maintain control over the sexuality of the women who, it is thought, ought to be under his oversight. Ignoring Ishbaal's power to grant sexual access to Rizpah, Abner has simply taken that power upon himself, and, in the bargain, taken Rizpah *for* himself. Thus, we can suggest that Ishbaal reads Abner's sexual act:

Abner >> Rizpah

as a message of power, and specifically as a message of power in relation to Ishbaal, which can thus be represented graphically as follows:

Abner >> Rizpah >> Ishbaal

In the eyes of Ishbaal, Abner is asserting his power over Ishbaal by means of the sexual relation with Rizpah. He asserts his power to act as a sexual subject toward Rizpah irrespective of Ishbaal's wishes. Neither the narrator nor the two male characters appear to be interested in Rizpah's perspective upon these events. Instead, she serves within this text a function very similar to that served by the Levite's concubine: she is the means with which a message of power is communicated between two men. She is the 'conduit of their relationship' (Rubin 1975).

If we consider the possibility that Ishbaal focalizes Abner's sexual activity from this perspective, then his suspicion makes sense. Indeed, his attitude is quite similar to attitudes discussed by many of the anthropologists whose work I have already summarized. His question to Abner is an expression of the required vigilance toward the sexuality of the women of one's household. By confronting Abner, Ishbaal need not be interpreted as implying that Abner is plotting for the throne. The confrontation would instead be an entirely appropriate response from a man who, within a certain cluster of assumptions about gender, prestige, and sexual practice, wishes to assert that he can act appropriately with regard to the culturally defined protocols of gender performance.

This interpretation actually coheres well with Abner's heated reply. Part of the content of Abner's reply to Ishbaal is, precisely, that Ishbaal *is* dependent upon Abner's power, that Abner *does* have a certain power over Ishbaal which he will now use to Ishbaal's disadvantage. Far from being a disclaimer of innocence in the face of Ishbaal's 'unjustified' (Hertzberg 1964: 257) accusation, Abner's reply is a refusal to recognize Ishbaal's rights in this matter, and therefore a sort of counter-attack on Ishbaal's masculine honor. Abner points out that Ishbaal is dependent for his power upon Abner and is by no means the independent, assertive subject whose role he attempts to fill. Dependence upon the power and goodwill of another man is itself often a negative signifier of manhood (cf. Gilmore 1990: 49-50). The balance of power between Abner and Ishbaal is thus crucial here.

In other words, by claiming the right to arbitrate in the matter of Rizpah's sexuality, Ishbaal assumes one sort of power relation. By questioning Abner he does become, however briefly, a narrative subject. Demanding an account of Abner's motives, he implicitly shows himself worthy of recognition as someone to whom Abner must answer. Yet if Ishbaal attempts to assert his authority here, implying his right to give Rizpah as he pleases, Abner in effect robs Ishbaal of any power at all by pointing out that Ishbaal's power is entirely a function of Abner's loyalty to the house of Saul. Abner's angry reply presupposes a very different power relation from that implied by Ishbaal's question. If Abner chooses to take away his support from Ishbaal, giving it to David instead, then Ishbaal's attempt to secure his father's position is futile.

The two characters assume two different sorts of power relations, but both men assume that the matter of sexual contact with Rizpah is a locus for such a dispute to be decided. The question at stake here is the question of the relative power positions of Ishbaal and Abner, but the realm in which that question is raised is the realm of sexual activity, and in particular, the power to give and to take the sexuality of Rizpah. Rizpah, then, as sexual object, becomes entirely a signifier here, a signifier of the power relations between the two men, Abner and Ishbaal. The ideology at work is not, in my opinion, a 'custom' about monarchical legitimacy. It is rather a complex bundle of premises about masculinity, sexual practice, and prestige which the anthropological literature helps to clarify. It is not so much that, as a king, Ishbaal claims the right to the royal harem; rather, as *a man*, Ishbaal claims the right to dispose of the sexuality of the women of his household, a right that Abner denies.

Moreover, the dispute here is one which Abner wins. Ishbaal, the narrator tells us, is afraid to pursue the matter further. In this regard, his attitude is precisely the opposite of that competitive and assertive display which the anthropological discussions of notions of manhood, mentioned above, might have led us to expect. Thus, it seems possible that Ishbaal's inability to maintain the discussion with Abner might have been interpreted as an indication of his inability to embody what Michael Herzfeld has called the 'cultural poetics of manhood' (Herzfeld 1985). Ishbaal's timidity is contrasted with Abner's competence in the games of gender performance. This competence, embodied elsewhere by his military prowess but here by his interventions with a woman of Ishbaal's household, cannot but increase his prestige in the eyes of a particular audience. David himself probably embodies the views of an assumed (and perhaps predominantly male) audience when, hearing of Abner's death, he bewails the fact that a prince and a great man has fallen in Israel (2 Sam. 3.38).

Thus, the taking of a previous ruler's concubine is only one example of a larger field of struggle between men, a field in which sexual contact with women is a weapon. There is nothing inherent in a wife or concubine of Saul that would grant legitimacy upon the person who wishes to assume Saul's position. The relation is actually rather different: the person who wishes to assume Saul's position must show himself to be worthy of that position in the eyes of other men, by demonstrating within himself those qualities that are thought to be essential in a king. Among those qualities, one's status as a gendered subject seems to be important, and this status entails the ability to control sexual access to the women of one's household.

Within the larger narrative, of course, these events are only recounted in order to tell us how it came to be that David secured the throne of Israel. One of the obstacles in David's way is Ishbaal, and we see here how Ishbaal was removed. Thus, another effect of the story, read within the anthropological framework, would be to provide a justification for Ishbaal's removal. Ishbaal, after all, has been shown to be something less than a 'real man', someone not deserving of gender-based prestige and so, it would seem, not deserving of the throne of Israel, either.

2 Samuel 11–12

The story recounted in 2 Samuel 11 and 12 has attracted more attention, scholarly and otherwise, than either of the previous texts. Indeed, it contains what is possibly the most-discussed instance of sexual contact in the entire Hebrew Bible. In recent years the text has been a favorite object of analysis for scholars interested in literary approaches (see, for example, Gunn 1978; Fokkelman 1981: 51-93; Sternberg 1985: 186-229; Bal 1987: 10-36; Ackerman 1990; Linafelt 1992; Exum 1993: 170-201). While these readings have produced an abundance of interesting insights, however, less attention has been given to the cultural dynamics that helped to give the narrative the shape and structure which it now has.

The story is often referred to as the 'story of David and Bathsheba', but this gloss is not entirely indicative of the story's actual focus, since it seems to be Uriah rather than Bathsheba whose relations with David trouble Nathan, YHWH, and the narrator. Moreover, the use of the English word 'adultery' to characterize this story risks misunderstanding from the beginning unless the difference between biblical and modern views of 'adultery' is taken into account. 'Adultery' is conventionally used today to refer to a type of sexual transgression which involves one or more married persons. As such, it is used of both married men and married women without significant distinction, as in the following randomly chosen dictionary definition: 'voluntary sexual intercourse between a married man and someone other than his wife or between a married woman and someone other than her husband' (*Webster's New Collegiate Dictionary*, s.v. 'adultery'). The symmetry in this definition between 'married man' and 'married woman' is clear, and reflects widespread usage. In contemporary Western culture, either a married woman or a married man is considered to have committed adultery when she or he has sexual intercourse outside of the marital union, irrespective of the marital or social status of the other sexual partner.

Some scholars consider the biblical concept of adultery to be similar to the contemporary understanding, inasmuch as the former is considered applicable to married men and married women without significant distinction (see, for example, Fuller 1993: 10). However, several scholars argue that modern views of 'adultery' probably differ from biblical views (see, for example, Bird 1989: 77; Frymer-Kensky 1992: 191; Yee 1992: 198). Within the Hebrew Bible, a married woman who has sexual relations with any man other than her husband is considered guilty of a sexual misdeed, but a married man's guilt depends upon the identity of the female partner with whom he has sexual relations. Sexual contact with the wife of another man, for example, is considered a misdeed for both the male and the female partner, whereas sexual contact with a female prostitute or female slave by a married man is apparently not considered a sexual offense. The distinguishing feature between these two examples is the presence or absence of a male who has rights over the woman's sexuality, rights which are considered to have been violated. The sexual offense committed by a married man with another man's wife is not considered to be an offense against the adulterer's wife, but rather against another man, the husband of the female sexual partner. It is my argument here that this general symbolic structure underlies David's 'adultery', conceptualized primarily as an action taken against Uriah and not, for example, against the wives and concubines of David (cf. Leach 1969: 71).

David's prestige may be in question from the beginning of ch. 11. The story begins with a statement about its setting, specified in both a temporal and a spatial manner. Temporally, the story takes place 'at the return of the year', generally considered to be the spring, a time, we are told, when 'the kings go out'. This 'going out' of 'the kings' has most often been taken as a statement about the conventional time for warfare, so that the NRSV, for example, translates 'In the spring of the year, the time when kings go out to battle' (see also Hertzberg 1964: 303; but cf. McCarter 1984: 285). On this understanding, the temporal indication tells us something about kingship norms. Kingship is associated with warfare, and kings normally take up their war-making activities in the spring (referring, apparently, to the beginning of the dry season). From the beginning, then, the story is linked specifically to 'political' issues, namely, issues of monarchy and warfare.

Spatially, the story takes place in Jerusalem, where David remains while Joab, his officers, and 'all Israel' lay siege to the Ammonite city of Rabbah. The spatial contrast between David and the other men of Israel is significant (cf. Bal 1987: 23, 31; Sternberg 1985: 193-95). Kings go to war at this time of year, but David remains in Jerusalem, even as other Israelites are sent out to battle Israel's enemies. The contrast between what kings do in the spring and what David does during this particular spring can lead to an evaluation of David. However, the nature of the evaluation depends upon the relative importance attached to military bravery and participation by the story's audience.

If the previous narratives of the Deuteronomistic History and of David's story are any indication of the general ideological assumptions about warfare which prevailed in the group(s) among which these texts were produced, it seems difficult to escape the conclusion that the contrast would have signified negatively in regard to David's character. While there are portions of the Hebrew Bible which speak critically of certain aspects of warfare, the books of the Deuteronomistic History tend to place a high value upon it, so long as the war is being carried out under particular approved conditions.[9] If war is being waged against an enemy of the Israelites, such as, in this case, the Ammonites, then participation in such a venture is generally approved. Bravery and success in battle are motivations for praise, as illustrated elsewhere by, for example, the significant contrast between Saul and David in 1 Sam. 18.6-9 concerning who has killed the most enemies. One's participation in and skill at warfare seem to have been criteria for the evaluation of one's prestige, at least for men,[10] and David's own reputation in the past had been affected positively by his successful demonstration of such qualities. Indeed, at this point in the narrative, David himself has just been represented as having led the Israelite army in the successful attack upon the Arameans allied with the Ammonites (2 Sam. 10.17-18).

In ch. 11, however, the picture of David is very different. We have a specification that David is not involved in a war being carried out by his army, even though, as king, his presence in battle might have been expected. Within a certain semiotics of bravery, David falls under suspicion of weakness and cowardice. It is even possible, in the light of our previous discussion of gender-based prestige and also in the light of ancient Near Eastern associations between warfare and masculinity (see Day 1991: 142-43), that his honor as a man is in doubt. In a cultural context in which an aggressive and competitive display of masculinity is valued, David's location in Jerusalem casts him in a negative light.

David might initially seem to be removed from any issues of power as well. If power struggles are present, they would appear to be located elsewhere, namely, at the battlefield from which David is absent. However, this first impression is countered by a careful consideration of the account of David and Bathsheba. For between the two characters, David and Bathsheba, power is both present and, within the discourse, quite unevenly distributed.

One afternoon, David rises from his couch for a stroll on the roof of his house (a roof which will become significant for another sexual relation in

9.   There is an enormous body of literature on biblical attitudes toward warfare. For a recent study of the problem, see Niditch 1993.

10.   Though perhaps, occasionally, for women as well, if the praise for Jael which we find in Judg. 5 is any indication (cf. Bal 1988a).

2 Sam. 16). The impression of a leisurely king reinforces the initial contrast between David and the men who are fighting the Ammonites with Joab. From his position on the roof David sees a woman whose identity is, as yet, unknown to either David or the reader. We see the woman with David. She is bathing, and she is very beautiful. The woman is thus an object of focalization, a focalization of which David is the subject. The relation between David's vision, the woman's beauty, and subsequent events shows that she is also the object of David's desire.

We are told absolutely nothing, however, about what the woman sees. We do not know, for example, if she sees David, and there is no hint in the text that such might be the case. Thus, there is no indication that the woman might be seducing David, although some commentators have indicated as much (see, for example, Hertzberg 1964: 309). Instead, the initiative comes entirely from David. He inquires who she is and, upon receiving the answer to his question, he sends messengers 'and he took her (ויקחה)'.

David is the subject of these actions as well. Although messengers are involved, they act only in relation to David's monologic command, as does Bathsheba (cf. Bal 1987: 28-29). The only point at which Bathsheba might be considered a subject is when she comes to the palace (ותבוא אליו). Bailey has suggested on the basis of Bathsheba's coming to the palace that she is an active, willing participant and partner in the deed that follows (Bailey 1990: 88). However, subject-position (she is indeed the subject of this single verb) has to be evaluated in terms of the relative social status and power held by the two characters in question. David is a king while Bathsheba is an inhabitant of David's domain, and this relation of power is crucial for our understanding of her action here. Bathsheba's action is no independent initiative (unlike David's), but the response to a royal command.

This distinction is important for an evaluation of thematic readings of this story. Once the difference in the social roles of the two characters is taken into account, it becomes difficult to argue that the woman actively brings about, in any way, the events that follow. It will be recalled that Blenkinsopp (1966) argued for the existence of a theme here, a theme summarized by the phrase 'the woman who brings death'. Yet this formulation of the theme places the woman in the position of subject. In fact, the relations represented in the text are quite different. The male king is the subject and the woman is the object. It is a *man* who brings about death in this story, and he brings about the death of *another man*.

The bringing of death is thus largely a homosocial affair.

The narrator of this story specifically notes the sexual contact which takes places between David and Bathsheba. The woman comes to David, in response to his royal command, 'and he lay with her' (וישכב עמה, v. 4). We can represent the situation graphically as follows:

David >> Bathsheba
male >> female

The male character is once again the subject of the sexual act, the female character the object. The sexual contact is stated specifically by the narrator, in distinction from the 2 Samuel 3 passage, but only briefly. There is no description of what takes place, no mention of the thoughts of either character. Nevertheless, the sexual act might seem to be a functional event. The eventual consequences of this act, after all, are quite significant, not only for the passages which follow immediately but also for events that follow at a much greater distance, as one of the characters (Nathan, speaking for YHWH) accurately predicts. The brief contact produces murder, prophetic and divine judgment, and, according to the prophetic speech, continuing warfare in the house of David.

On the other hand, Nathan's important speech does not follow immediately after the sexual contact with Bathsheba, but rather after the murder of Uriah. Thus, one must consider the possibility that it is this action taken toward the male character (Uriah) which is the primary motivation for YHWH's rebuke, and not the sexual act itself. As we shall see, the parable told by Nathan confirms this possibility. Such divine displeasure toward David as the text actually states is described only after the murder, and not after the sexual relation per se. It is therefore not certain that the sexual relation alone, recounted outside of the context of treachery and murder, would produce exactly the same result.

In the short term, David apparently tries to keep the sexual contact a secret. However, Bathsheba turns out to be pregnant and, upon hearing this news, David orders Joab to send her husband, Uriah, back from the battlefield. David is once again a subject, but acting here in relation to a male object. If we restate the subject–object relation so that it represents, not sexual contact, but power over another person (the latter, I have argued, sometimes implied by the former), we can represent it as follows:

David >> Uriah
male >> male

This relation, which David's command assumes, turns out to be the primary relation in the story. The focus is upon this relation, however, because its success is called into question. The plot revolves around the fact that Uriah resists the logic of the social roles of king and soldier upon which David relies.

David's intentions are never stated directly, but, as inferred from the text, they are almost universally agreed upon. After first engaging Uriah in a conversation about the war with the Ammonites, David orders Uriah to 'Go down to your house, and wash your feet'. The command is obviously, on one level, an explicit order for Uriah to rest and refresh himself. Nevertheless, by returning to his house, Uriah will also be close to Bathsheba. The possibility is raised that Uriah will have sexual relations with his wife. If, so soon after David's sexual relations with the woman, Uriah can be compelled to fulfill the role which David has usurped, David's actions will remain hidden. The child that is born will be attributed to Uriah. That David feels compelled to resort to this subterfuge already alerts us to an interesting fact about sexual practice which is presupposed here: the king cannot simply do what he wants, so far as sexual relations are concerned. There are limits placed upon his 'rights' in this matter.

Some scholars have suggested that the reference to 'washing the feet' is being used here to hint at sexual intercourse (McCarter 1984: 286; Hertzberg 1964: 310). As has often been noted, 'feet' seems to be used in some instances in the Hebrew Bible euphemistically, referring to the genitals (cf. Ruth 3.4, 7; Ezek. 16.25). In any case, Uriah makes the possibility of intercourse explicit when David asks him why he refuses to spend the night in his own house. In v. 11, Uriah retorts,

> The ark and Israel and Judah dwell in booths,[11] and my lord Joab and the servants of my lord are camping in the field. So should I go to my house, to eat and to drink, and to lie with my wife? As you live, and as your soul lives, I will not do this thing.

Now this speech amounts to nothing less than a rebuttal of the king's command to Uriah. However, the explanation which Uriah gives seems to be a compelling one, for David refrains from trying to persuade (still less to order) Uriah to go down to his house.

Commentators have generally explained the logic of Uriah's response

---

11. It is possible that 'booths' ought to be taken as a place name here, and translated 'Succoth' (so, for example, McCarter 1984: 287).

to David by referring to a set of relations between sexual contact and warfare spelled out elsewhere in the Hebrew Bible, notably in 1 Samuel 21. There, the priest refuses to give holy bread to David and his soldiers until he is assured that they have not had sexual relations with women. David assures the priest that, as is generally the case on military expeditions, the young men with him have refrained from any sort of contact with women and so are 'holy'. Some sort of link is clearly being made in 1 Samuel 21 between the ritual purity required for warfare and abstention from sexual contact with women.

This requirement is itself an interesting case of the differences in attitudes toward sexual practice between the biblical texts and the modern world. Scholars have proposed that the same convention of purity might have given logic to Uriah's response to David, so far as sexual relations with Bathsheba were concerned (see, for example, McCarter 1984: 286). According to this interpretation, Uriah is refusing to have sexual relations with his wife because it would break the ritual purity required of soldiers during warfare.

While this is generally plausible within the context of the Hebrew Bible, it is likely that more is going on here. For one thing, Uriah does not so much renounce sexual contact in and of itself (although that is certainly included) as the comforts of home in general. It is not only sexual contact with his wife, but also eating, drinking, and sleeping in his house that Uriah mentions in his reply. The sexual aspect strikes us as relevant, of course, because it is that aspect which holds the key to David's planned cover-up. For Uriah, however, the sexual element is only one part of a larger concern for *solidarity* with his counterparts at the front (see Bal 1987: 30-31). This sort of betrayal of his fellow soldiers, at the moment at which cooperation and solidarity in the face of a common enemy seem to be called for, would surely be considered a serious breach of honor on Uriah's part. To act in such a manner would be shameful.

The reply, understood in this way, highlights again the contrast between David and the other men of Israel, represented here by Uriah. For this portrait of a leisurely life at home, enjoyed while one's comrades are at war, a life which Uriah rejects, underscores the spatio-temporal location of David specified at the beginning of the story. That which Uriah rejects as a point of honor is precisely the life which David leads at the beginning of the chapter, including, ironically enough, sexual contact with Uriah's own wife. We can even suggest that Uriah's honor contrasts with David's dishonor, perhaps with his shame, and that this is precisely part of his function within the story: he highlights the characteristics which David should, but does not, display.

Uriah goes on to resist yet again David's plotting, this time after David sees to it that Uriah becomes drunk.[12] Again, however, Uriah refrains from going home. Finally, another solution is found to David's dilemma. Using his powers as king once again, David sends a command to Joab which amounts to a death sentence for Uriah. At a moment of heated battle, Joab and the other soldiers are to pull back from Uriah, leaving him alone and at the mercy of Israel's enemy. In a scene with some parallels elsewhere in ancient literature (cf. McCarter 1984: 287), it is Uriah who, unknowingly, carries the letter containing David's message to Joab, thereby facilitating his own death under David's order. The situation here is ironic, inasmuch as Uriah dies due to a lack of solidarity on the part of his male colleagues, and particularly Joab. The same individual who refused to spend the night in his house while his comrades, including explicitly 'my lord Joab', slept on the ground, dies when Joab, under orders from David, places him strategically at 'the place where he knew there were strong [Ammonite] warriors' (v. 16) and then calls the other Israelite soldiers back. Bathsheba, informed of the situation, mourns for her husband's death, and there seems to be no reason to doubt her sincerity. Her dealings with David have, after all, been entirely at David's command. After her period of mourning has passed, David takes Bathsheba as his wife, and she subsequently gives birth to David's son.

The key to understanding this incident lies within ch. 12. David's plans seem to have been carried out more or less successfully until the narrator notes, at the very end of ch. 11, that 'the thing that David had done was evil in the eyes of YHWH' (v. 27). Here we see David's actions with YHWH, who is thus explicitly a focalizing character ('in the eyes of YHWH'), and David's actions are focalized negatively. If ch. 11 as a whole contains few explicit evaluative comments, this comment casts David's actions retrospectively in a negative light, since YHWH is the character whose focalization is likely to be accepted by most readers.

The reasons for YHWH's displeasure are generally assumed to be self-evident: 'adultery' and murder. However, the statement of YHWH's

---

12. The examples of Lot (Gen. 19.30-38) and Boaz (Ruth 3.7) may indicate some sort of association between drunkenness and a susceptibility to sexual desire in Israelite thought which might have given a certain logic to David's scheme.

displeasure at the end of ch. 11 does not specify the criteria for the focalization, which is to say, the standards by which David is evaluated. There actually seem to be several dimensions to YHWH's response, as mediated through Nathan the prophet in ch. 12, and these need to be examined closely for an understanding of the ideology of sexual contact at work here.

Nathan, who is sent by YHWH and thus seems to represent the opinion of the divine character, tells David a story. It contains two principal characters who are contrasted with one another in economic terms: one is rich, the other is poor. The differential in economic status is explicitly spelled out, and clearly considered relevant. The rich man has many flocks and herds, but the poor man has only one female lamb, which is said specifically to be 'like a daughter' to him. When a traveler visits the rich man, the rich man, not wanting to kill one of his own many animals, takes and kills the lamb which belongs to the poor man. At this point in the telling of the tale David interjects angrily that the man who had stolen the lamb deserved to die.

Nathan responds that the rich man is, in fact, David himself, and the parallels between the story which Nathan has told and the events in ch. 11 become clear. If David is the rich man, Uriah is the poor man, and it is these two male characters who become the primary human figures in Nathan's retelling. Bathsheba, on the other hand, is signified by a lamb—a beloved lamb to be sure, but an animal none the less. Now it would be ill-advised to jump from this symbolism to the simple conclusion that women were considered to be, more or less, in the position of cattle in ancient Israel. However, it is true that the relation between Uriah and Bathsheba is signified by the relation between a man and his animal, that the singular animal of the poor man is contrasted with the herds of the rich man, and that David's adultery is represented in terms of property theft. The fact that only David and Uriah are represented in the parable by human characters indicates that they are the characters with which Nathan (and by extension YHWH) is primarily concerned.

The symbolism should not necessarily be seen as an accurate *reflection* of the roles which women held in the society which produced the text, however. Once again, the question of the subject becomes relevant. The discourse which this text constitutes seems to be a male-centered discourse, and women are focalized not out of an interest in their 'actual' status and power but, rather, in terms of their relation to a homosocial network. From the perspective of the male–male relation, women are seen as objects over which men can and do struggle.

The fact that the lamb is, in turn, compared with a daughter is also significant. The comparison is generally assumed to be relevant only as an index of the affection which the poor man holds for his lamb. However, we have already seen in our review of the anthropological literature that the connotations of 'daughter' are not always identical to connotations associated with Anglo-American concepts of family relations. Daughters are significant in some cultural contexts not only because one might have affection for them, but also because they are thought to contain within themselves a feature which comes to serve as a sort of symbolic capital for their male kinsmen: their sexual purity. In this regard, the taking of a lamb who is 'like a daughter' and the taking of a wife for sexual purposes can be seen as not altogether different actions, particularly from the perspective of the male subjects involved, that is, the man who takes and the man from whom the female objects are taken. In both instances, a female serves as the conduit of a relation between the two men, and the sexual availability of the woman taken is an issue.

The point of the parable seems relatively clear. It is dishonorable for a rich man who possesses many herds and flocks to take the one sheep of a poor man. The two men do not stand on a level playing field. They are not equivalent characters. Hence, any sort of notion of 'contest' is meaningless here. Bourdieu (1979) has argued that transactions of male honor presuppose a more or less equivalent claim to prestige on the part of the parties involved. If two men are obviously contrasted in terms of some significant social differential, then the more powerful man who chooses to provoke a weaker man risks dishonoring himself. The transaction that takes place is not actually a contest for honor and prestige, but is much closer to abuse and exploitation. Others have made similar points, with Campbell noting in particular the dishonor which one brings upon oneself by exploiting the poor, who, significantly, are sometimes defined by the fact that they have fewer animals than the rich (Campbell 1964: 293). Something similar seems to have taken place between David and Uriah. David, as king, has power over Uriah from the beginning, power which he is willing to use but also to abuse in order to fulfill his desires. Here, the power has been abused to the point of murdering an innocent man.

Now there is little evidence here of disapproval of the traffic in women as a male practice. That men struggling with one another for power and precedence might use women to further their ends seems to be accepted, at least to a certain extent. Indeed, and this is crucial, YHWH is shown to have been a player in this game. David's accumulated power up to this point is signified by, among other things, the fact that he has obtained the wives of his predecessor, and it is precisely YHWH who has 'given' these women to David. YHWH, in other words, is a *subject* of the traffic in women:

> Thus says YHWH, the God of Israel: I anointed you king over Israel, and I delivered you from the hand of Saul, and *I gave you* the house of your lord, *and the wives of your lord* into your bosom, and I gave you the house of Israel and of Judah. (2 Sam. 12.7b-8a, my emphasis)

The use of women as symbolic capital, circulating among men and used as signifiers of male power, is never questioned as a general principle. On the contrary, it is a process in which YHWH has been actively involved (cf. Schwartz 1991: 47; Linafelt 1992: 105).

Why then, exactly, is YHWH angry with David? It is clearly not the taking of another man's wife, in and of itself, since YHWH has been complicit in such activities himself. It is, rather, the particular circumstances under which this particular woman was taken. David is faulted here for having failed to play by the rules of the game, even though neither the rules nor the game itself are questioned. It is not honorable to have taken the wife of a man over whom one clearly has such a significant advantage. Indeed, the dynamic at work is probably not so different from that expressed in the common injunction, found frequently even among schoolchildren, to 'pick on someone your own size'. The incident represented here was no challenge among men struggling for precedence, in which each could potentially be the victor. Such had been the case with David and Saul, and such seems to be the normal protocol of challenge and response which anthropologists writing on honor and shame have emphasized. This incident, instead, was an exploitative manipulation of a person whose political subordination to David was never in question. Moreover, while it might seem clear enough to us that Bathsheba, as well as Uriah, was being exploited, the parable indicates that such was not the major thrust of YHWH's response. It is the exploitation of Uriah rather than that of Bathsheba which concerns Nathan and YHWH.

David's problem is not, therefore, that he has entered the arena of sex, honor, and power, but that he has done so outside of particular conventional conditions. Had Bathsheba been the means with which to challenge a man who was a true social rival of David's, or who was in some manner acting dishonorably himself, it is quite possible that the response of YHWH would have been altogether different. The parable indicates, however, that the difference between David and Uriah, a difference signified by the opposition 'rich man/poor man', was a crucial component of YHWH's displeasure.

While the story of Nabal and Abigail indicates that bloodguilt may have been one issue raised by Uriah's death (cf. 2 Sam. 25.2-42), Nathan's parable does not stress or even mention the murder at all, but only the social differential between the two men, one of whom steals from the other. The taking of another man's wife seems to be an acceptable message of power so long as one honors the contextual constraints, such as challenging only a man who might actually be considered a rival.[13] David, then, is not condemned for what we would today consider a 'sexual offense', but rather for transgressing the conventional structures of the male contest for honor and power and disregarding the rights of an honorable man fighting at David's command against a traditional Israelite enemy. As punishment, YHWH decrees that David will himself become a victim of the use of sexual contact in the competitive traffic in women. Hence, we see once again that the use of women by men in male struggles for power is itself not challenged, but rather utilized, by the divine character upon whom the authors of these texts projected their values.

Briefly, then, the dynamics of the passage can be summarized. David begins under a shadow of suspicion, and proceeds to carry out what could be, *under certain circumstances*, an index of masculine honor and prestige: he desires and obtains sexual relations with a woman.

David >> Bathsheba
male >> female

In this case, however, he has chosen the wife of a soldier, someone who is, under the circumstances (a time of war against the Ammonites), acting in an approved manner. He takes advantage of the power he has over Uriah and abuses this power to the point of murder. His victim is arguably acting more honorably than David even before the sexual contact with Bathsheba, simply by being on the battlefront at a time of year

---

13. As we know in the wake of speech-act theory, messages only communicate under certain conditions; 'speech-acts' only succeed in relatively well-defined contexts (cf. Austin 1975). The point being made here is that the same context-dependence characterizes 'sex acts' by which men communicate with other men.

when 'kings go out to war'. Ultimately, as the parable makes clear by representing Bathsheba as a lamb over which two men dispute, Bathsheba comes to serve as the conduit of a relationship between two men:

David >> Bathsheba >> Uriah
male >> female >> male

We see once again a recurring dynamic at work, a dynamic present in the previous two stories. The nature of David's offense is constituted by relations of power, honor, and gender.

2 Samuel 13

Like the story of David, Bathsheba, and Uriah in 2 Samuel 11, the story of Amnon, Tamar, and Absalom in 2 Samuel 13 has received a great deal of attention from scholars associated with literary interpretations of the Bible (see, for example, Conroy 1978; Fokkelman 1981: 99-125; Trible 1984: 37-63; Bar-Efrat 1989: 239-82; Van Dijk-Hemmes 1989). The story is a good case for literary analysis, containing, for example, some of the most interesting instances of characterization to be found in the Hebrew Bible. The primary 'sexual' element in this chapter, the rape of Tamar by her half-brother Amnon, has long been recognized as an important part of the story. However, the story's relation to cultural assumptions about sexual practice that may be illuminated by anthropology requires further analysis.

The story begins with a statement that 'Absalom, the son of David, had a beautiful sister whose name was Tamar; and Amnon the son of David loved her' (13.1). The fact that both Absalom and David are mentioned before either Tamar or Amnon, in spite of the fact that the latter two characters dominate the first portion of the narrative, is significant (cf. Bar-Efrat 1989: 240-41). The motivation for the telling of the events that take place between Amnon and Tamar seems to be an interest in the role of these events within the story of Absalom and David. While Amnon is killed before the end of the chapter, and Tamar disappears from the narrative stage even sooner, the relations between the two characters mentioned first—Absalom and David—will be narrated for several more chapters. The story of Amnon and Tamar thus functions in part to characterize Absalom and David.

The fact that Tamar is characterized first of all as *Absalom's sister* is important. It has already been pointed out that sisters play a particularly potent symbolic role in male–male relations in a number of societies. In particular, the ability to guard against threats to a sister's sexual purity or to avenge sexual misconduct against one's sister is often an index of masculine honor. 'Vigilance' (Schneider 1971) in the face of threats to the sexual purity of a sister is a significant component of the ideology underlying this text as well. By calling attention to Tamar's relation of kinship with Absalom, the narrative prepares a reader for Absalom's response, since readers would assume that a brother ought to respond to the rape of his sister in socially approved ways.

Amnon, we are told, loves Tamar so severely that he becomes ill. However, according to the narrator, Amnon does not see that he can do anything about his desire, since Tamar is a בתולה (13.2). It should be stressed that the kinship relation between Amnon and Tamar (she is his half-sister) is not specified as an obstacle to the prince. 'Incest' does not seem to be the primary sexual issue at stake in the story, although the incestuous relation may have intensified an already volatile situation, that is, the rape of another man's sister. Rather, Tamar's status as בתולה seems to be more important than her status as Amnon's half-sister in keeping him from carrying out his desires, and it is in fact focalized by him as a hindrance ('because she was a בתולה and it seemed impossible in the eyes of Amnon to do anything to her').

The term בתולה has traditionally been translated into English as 'virgin' (by, for instance, McCarter [1984: 314]; Hertzberg [1964: 320]; Trible [1984: 38-39]; Bar-Efrat [1989: 243-44], as well as most English versions). This description of Tamar can be taken together with the previous description of Tamar as *Absalom's* sister. Indeed, a notation of Tamar's physical virginity coheres with the connotations of Tamar's kinship relation. The anthropological discussions of the significance of the 'virginity' of sisters, daughters, and other kinswomen (see for example Schneider 1971; Ortner 1978; Giovannini 1987; Delaney 1991: 40, 97) shed light on the effect which sexual contact with Tamar might have on the honor and reputation of her male relatives. A woman's virginity is often a fact about the woman which her kinsmen feel the need to protect as a point of their own honor.

While the translation 'virgin' seems plausible enough here, however, and is in fact the translation which I prefer, a number of questions have been raised about the precise status signified by בתולה, which according to some commentators may represent not so much 'virginity' per se but rather a phase of a young woman's life, a phase occurring between the onset of puberty and either marriage or the birth of the first child.

Several arguments have been given to support this second interpretation (see, for what follows, Wenham 1972; Day 1989: 59; 1991: 144-45; Tsevat 1977; Bal 1988b: 46-48).

First, the terms בתולה and בתולים are sometimes accompanied by an additional notation that the young woman in question has not had sexual relations (see, for instance, Gen. 24.16; Judg. 11.37-39; 21.12). It has been argued that this notation is redundant if בתולה means 'virgin'. Secondly, evidence from other Semitic texts indicates that the cognate terms may not always mean 'virgin' in a technical sense, but rather 'young woman'. Thirdly, it has been argued that in some instances the biblical term בתולה simply cannot mean 'virgin'. More specifically, Joel 1.8 asks its audience to lament 'like a *betulah*' (כבתולה) mourning 'for the husband of her youth' (על־בעל נעוריה). The two terms בתולה and בעל seem contradictory if the former term in fact means 'virgin'. In addition, Est. 2.17-19 seems to refer to the young women who have each spent a night with King Ahasuerus as בתולות even after they have had sexual relations with him.

On the basis of these sorts of arguments, Wenham goes so far as to suggest that no occurrence of the term בתולה in the Hebrew Bible actually needs to be understood as a technical term for 'virgin'. Even Deut. 22.13-21, in which a husband claims not to have found evidence of his wife's בתולים at the time of marriage, is reinterpreted by Wenham on the basis of his view that בתולה signifies 'a woman of marriageable age'. The parents of the accused bring out the בתולים of their daughter to counter the husband's charges. This latter term is generally translated 'tokens of virginity' (BDB: 144) or 'evidence of virginity' (NRSV) and is usually taken as a reference to bloodstained bedclothes or garments from the wedding night of the younger couple. Even commentators who are inclined to interpret most instances of בתולה as 'young woman' sometimes concede that Deuteronomy 22 is concerned with physical virginity (see, for example, Tsevat 1977). Wenham, however, noting the ease with which the parents' evidence could be manufactured, questions the plausibility of this scenario and suggests instead that we are to think here of a garment or cloth stained with the young woman's menstrual blood, such blood being proof that the woman had reached the state of nubility which made her suitable for marriage.

We may start with Wenham's discussion of Deuteronomy 22 in evaluating the force of these arguments and their implications for our passage. In spite of Wenham's reinterpretation, Deuteronomy 22 does indeed seem to refer to 'virginity'. While it is true that deception on the part of the woman's parents can be imagined (and this is true, it should be pointed out, even if Wenham is correct about the meaning of בתולה, so that the point does not really support his argument), the custom is nevertheless known actually to exist and has been described by anthropologists in relation to contexts in which virginity is at stake (see, for example, Delaney 1991: 146; Giovannini 1987: 61). This fact does not in itself determine the meaning of the Hebrew term בתולה, of course, but it does undermine Wenham's suggestion that the scenario is implausible due to the possibility of the falsification of evidence.

Moreover, it has to be noted that if the woman's parents are unable to produce evidence of their daughter's בתולים, she is punished with death (22.21). This punishment seems unlikely if, as Wenham claims, menstruation is at stake, for menstruation will in most instances still occur in the future. A failure to menstruate scarcely seems like the sort of problem for which a young woman might be executed.

In addition, her punishment is explicitly justified on the grounds that she has 'committed a disgraceful act (נבלה) in Israel, to whore (לזנות) the house of her father'. This notation is surely a reference to premarital sexual activity. זנה signifies sexual contact, either literally or metaphorically (as in the case of religious unfaithfulness), and נבלה is in a number of instances, including the story of Tamar with which we are here concerned and the story of Judges 19 which we have already discussed, linked to sexual misconduct. The most plausible way of explaining the passage in Deuteronomy 21 is that the woman's premarital sexual activity has made it impossible for her parents to produce the בתולים, so that in fact the younger husband is asserting, correctly, that the woman was not a בתולה—a 'virgin'—at the time of their marriage. Starting from this case, then, we can argue that בתולה can certainly mean 'virgin' in at least some biblical instances.

Since many occurrences of the term appear in contexts (including that of 2 Sam. 13) where either of the two suggested meanings—'virgin' or 'young woman of marriageable age'—would make sense, one must ask whether there are sufficient examples of instances in which בתולה simply cannot mean 'virgin' to justify the assumption that 'young woman of marriageable age' is the primary meaning. Unfortunately, the answer to this question depends in part, as is so often true of philological disputes, on the interpretation of passages about which there is disagreement. Nevertheless, the examples appealed to by Wenham and others are not necessarily definitive. Est. 2.17-19, for example, is less relevant than

Wenham implies. The narrator can be taken as referring to the young women as בתולות retrospectively, that is, in terms of their specified status at the moment they were brought into the king's bedchamber. Joel 1.8, which refers to the woman lamenting for the בעל of her youth, does seem to be more difficult for the assumption that בתולה most often means 'virgin', but the difficulty is not insurmountable. On the contrary, some interpreters of Joel 1 have suggested that the young woman is lamenting for the man to whom she has been betrothed, a man who has, however, been killed prior to the consummation of marriage (see, for example, Wolff 1977: 30-31).

So far as the redundancy of such passages as Gen. 24.16, Judg. 11.37-39 and 21.12 is concerned, the argument runs up against the methodological problem of the significance of repetition in biblical narrative. Biblical literature is so frequently repetitive that literary critics have been compelled to offer an explanation of its significance (see, for example, Alter 1981: 88-113; Sternberg 1985: 365-440). Not only does this frequency make one hesitant to rule out the possibility that בתולה can mean 'virgin' on the basis of the supposed 'redundancy' of three passages; the literary-critical discussions might lead one to the opposite conclusion that the repetition is deployed in order to *emphasize* the virginity of the young women in question. In other words, repetition may function 'to draw the reader's attention to an important point' (Bar-Efrat 1989: 117). Once again, this fact in itself does not prove that בתולה means 'virgin' rather than 'woman of marriageable age'; it simply suggests that the question of redundancy, far from eliminating the meaning 'virginity' when the word is accompanied by a notation that the woman in question has not had sexual relations, could on the contrary be used to argue that the woman's virginity is a central point to which attention is being drawn.

Consequently, one is left primarily with the argument that, in other Semitic languages, terms which are cognate with בתולה do not always (but may on occasion) function as technical terms for virginity. This argument simply brings us back to the less-than-novel suggestion that one must determine on the basis of context whether בתולה refers to the physical state of never having had sexual intercourse or to the age-group in which a woman is ready to be married. Such a conclusion is reached by such commentators as, for instance, Tsevat (1977), who is generally inclined to see בתולה as a 'young woman' but who argues that in some instances (such as Deut. 22) it signifies virginity.

If the exact status of בתולה has to be determined by context, it should be noted that there are several points of contact between the scenario envisioned in Deuteronomy 22 and the plot of 2 Samuel 13. Both texts deal with a young woman who either is or is supposed to be a בתולה before marriage, both texts raise the question of illegitimate sexual activity (associated in both instances, as we shall see below, with the evaluative term נבלה) prior to marriage, and in both texts the male relatives of the woman make a public response to the situation: in spite of the mother's assistance in producing evidence in Deut. 22.14, it is the father alone who speaks in defense of his daughter in vv. 16-17 and whose house is said to be dishonored in v. 21 should בתולים prove to be lacking.

Indeed, the latter point coheres well with the socio-cultural assumptions that have been discussed throughout this study. In a recent discussion of the 'virgin' in ancient Israel which includes an interpretation of 2 Samuel 13, Victor Matthews and Don Benjamin hint at an important component of the significance of בתולה by calling attention not only to the philological question which has attached itself to the term—does it or does it not refer to 'virgo intacta'—but also to the social dimensions of the term (see Matthews and Benjamin [eds.] 1993: 176-86). While the discussion of Matthews and Benjamin is occasionally prone to unsupported conclusions (such as their assertion that Amnon rapes Tamar in part to assert his right, rather than the right of Absalom, to the throne of Israel), it nevertheless makes a crucial point, namely, that the בתולה is particularly susceptible to being caught up in disputes about male honor.

This fact is implied in Deuteronomy 22 where, I have suggested, literal 'virginity' is in fact signified. The accusation of a lack of בתולים in the young woman is seen in part as a reflection of the honor of the woman's father, for it is the father rather than the daughter who receives the fine from the husband if the accusation should turn out to be false. Moreover, if the accusation is true, the woman is killed at the entrance to her father's house, for she has done a disgraceful thing 'to whore the house of her father' (לזנות בית אביה): it is her father's house against which her action is considered a misdeed. As we shall see, the reputation of male kinsmen also seems to be at stake in 2 Samuel 13.

Thus, even if it is true that, in some instances, בתולה can refer simply to a 'young woman of marriageable age', the similarities between Deuteronomy 22 and 2 Samuel 13 make the translation 'virgin' the more plausible rendering in the latter case as in the former. Tamar's qualification as בתולה is not only an indication of her unavailability for sexual relations with Amnon, although it is explicitly that. It also indicates Tamar's status as a young woman who stands in a particular position which is overdetermined by male concerns for honor and reputation.

With the help of his friend and cousin Jonadab, Amnon devises a plot to obtain Tamar. He pretends to be ill, and asks his father to allow Tamar to come and make cakes 'in my sight' so that 'I will eat from her hand' (13.6). David grants Amnon's request, and sends Tamar to Amnon's house. As was true of Bathsheba, the first actual appearance of the female character on the narrative stage grants her only a very circumscribed subject-position. She does act, but under the orders of her father the king rather than from her own initiative.

However, David's own narrative role is somewhat complicated here as well. While he is the immediate source of the order to Tamar, he is also falling prey to Amnon's plot. He sends Tamar because Amnon has requested that he do so, and David seems to have little sense that a plot is being carried out. Ultimately, then, David is characterized together with Tamar as an unwitting object of Amnon's scheme. Indeed, since David is actually the character who has the power to grant Amnon's request, his failure to recognize Amnon's true intentions may be thematized. Tamar follows the order of her father the king, a response which, if limited in power, is easily understood. David, on the other hand, fails to recognize that he is being fooled, and the result is a negative opinion of the king's ability to perceive the actual state of affairs.

Tamar's actions in preparing the cakes for Amnon are described in considerable detail. Indeed, the amount of detail used in this description is quite remarkable for a biblical narrative. Part of the effect of this detail is the sense that *we are seeing Tamar along with Amnon*. Amnon seems to be a focalizing subject here, having specifically requested (as Jonadab specifically suggested, and David specifically commanded) that Tamar prepare the cakes 'in his sight' (vv. 5, 6). Tamar is described as the object of his gaze, as well as of his schemes.

Amnon, in contrast, continues to be the primary narrative subject here. Having tricked David into doing that which he wishes, having caused Tamar to come to him, and having watched her prepare the food, in v. 9 he sends everyone out of his chamber except for Tamar. In response to his order, Tamar brings the cakes to Amnon, and at this point he grabs Tamar and, asserting once again his subject-status over her, commands her, 'Come, lie with me, my sister'.

Tamar, however, resists Amnon's advances:

> But she said to him, 'No, my brother, do not afflict me, because it is not
> done thus in Israel. Do not do this disgraceful thing. And I, where will I
> carry my shame? And you will surely be like one of the disgraceful men
> in Israel. Now please speak to the king; for he will not withhold me from
> you' (2 Sam. 13.12-13).

The language used in this reply is similar to language we have already
seen in Judges 19. There, the host refers to the intentions of the men of
Gibeah with the same words used by Tamar to refer to Amnon's
intentions here: 'Do not do this disgraceful thing'. The Hebrew phrase
which I have translated using the English phrase 'this disgraceful thing'
(את־הנבלה הזאת) is an evaluative phrase, and therefore implies someone's
point of view, a perspective from which the act in question is considered
negatively. Just as the host in Judges 19 focalizes the intended act of the
men of Gibeah for them and shows them that it is shameful, so now
Tamar focalizes the intended act of Amnon, showing him that his
intentions are shameful as well.

However, the linguistic similarity between these two cases reveals at
the same moment a striking difference. The host in Judges 19, as we have
already seen, offers two young women as a substitute for his male guest
and tells the men to 'humble them' (וענו אותם, Judg. 19.24), using to
signify the rape which he is *offering* the same *piel* verb (ענה) that Tamar
uses to refer to the rape which she is *attempting to prevent* (אל־תעני, 'do
not humble me', 2 Sam. 13.12). In the two cases, therefore, the connotations of הנבלה do not seem to be identical, in spite of the fact that rape is
an issue in both texts. Tamar uses the term to refer to her own rape,
which is to say, the rape of a female character, whereas the male host in
Gibeah specifically recommends the rape of two female characters *as an
alternative to* the נבלה which he tries to prevent: the rape of a male
character.

It thus appears that Tamar does not focalize the event in question in
exactly the same manner as the host of Gibeah. She considers the rape
of young women to be a 'disgraceful thing' (נבלה). He considers the
rape of young women to be, if not exactly a positive thing, nevertheless
preferable to the 'disgraceful thing' (נבלה). The difference in positions of
focalization seems to be linked not only to the gender of the potential
objects of rape, but also to the gender of the two focalizing characters.

We can even suggest that the concubine and the host's daughter in
Judges 19 might have been plausibly represented as referring to their
own rape, rather than the rape of the Levite, as 'this disgraceful thing'

(את־הנבלה הזאת) had they been granted the position of focalizing subject. Their own opinion is simply not given, and seems to have been considered irrelevant. Tamar's discourse, however, does contain the focalization of a sexual act by a female character', and is exceptional in this regard. By comparing the two cases, we see the value of paying attention to instances in which the position of focalizing subject is *not* granted to this or that character, since such a narrative technique has specific (and sometimes ideological) effects. We can also see the value of Bal's point that it may be preferable to avoid general statements about *the* 'point of view' in a text and pay attention instead to the specific instances of focalization which give a narrative text its particular literary effects.

Tamar's speech also confirms that the particular deed which is most problematic in this passage is not incest (contra McCarter 1984: 324) but rather rape. Sexual contact per se between Amnon and Tamar is apparently not forbidden, or at least not unthinkable: if Amnon asks David, Tamar tells her brother, then surely David 'will not withhold me from you' (13.13). This statement may constitute evidence that assumptions about sexual practice which underlie biblical narratives are not always compatible with those underlying biblical laws, so that the critic cannot simply use, without reflection, the one to explain the other. Sexual relations between siblings are strictly forbidden in the Holiness Code (Lev. 18.9, 11; 20.17), and are cursed as well in the list of offenses found in Deuteronomy 27 (v. 22), hence within the boundaries of what is usually considered to be the introduction to the Deuteronomistic History. Yet Tamar's attempt to reason with Amnon here could only have made sense in a context in which liaisons between siblings were at least conceivable. It is therefore necessary to acknowledge a tension between the position represented by Tamar's words and that represented in the biblical legal discourse, without, however, denying that the rape of one's own sister might have been considered more reprehensible than the rape of another woman.[14]

Amnon does not listen to Tamar's pleas. 'Being stronger than she'

14. I see no reason to accept the argument of McCarter that, since Tamar would not have protested so vehemently and used such strong language about 'a simple rape…the sacrilege in the present passage is incest' (1984: 324). As I have already pointed out, the distinguishing characteristic of Tamar's language is precisely the fact that it is the only instance in the Deuteronomistic History where a woman's rape is focalized by the woman herself, which may very well help to account for the difference in language.

(2 Sam. 13.14), he rapes her. Here the power relations, on a quite physical level, between Amnon and Tamar are specific. Tamar has been brought to this point by Amnon's plots, but it is finally his sheer physical strength that overcomes her. What follows is, however, from Tamar's viewpoint, even worse.

After raping Tamar, Amnon is filled with hatred for her. In a quite descriptive turn of words, the narrator states that 'the hatred with which he hated her was greater than the love with which he had loved her' (v. 15). He orders her to leave. Once again Tamar pleads with Amnon, telling him that, in sending her away, he is committing a greater misdeed than the one he has already committed by raping her. Here the logic of the narrative *does* seem to cohere with the logic of legal discourse elsewhere in the Hebrew Bible. The general idea behind this statement is similar to the one found in, for example, Deut. 22.28-29: if a man rapes a 'virgin', he ought to marry her. The woman's desire in such a case is not considered by the law, and she is apparently forced to marry the man who has raped her. That Tamar should wish for such a thing at this point, and even characterize Amnon's refusal as a greater evil than the rape which preceded it, is at first baffling.

The logic displayed in the legal text may rest upon a concern about the impact of the loss of the woman's sexual purity upon future attempts to marry her. One wonders who the subject of this concern is. Where men place a high value on female sexual purity, it can be difficult to find a husband willing to marry a woman who is considered to be 'tainted' by the trace of the man who has been there before him. It is only a short step from formulating a 'solution' to this problem without inquiring about the feelings of the woman involved, as the law does, to assuming that the woman involved would consider the solution a suitable one, and write a story accordingly. We may have here the projection of an 'official' position via the voice of a female character.

On the other hand, one must consider the constraints under which a woman in this situation would have found herself. The fact of male dominance, the emphasis upon female sexual purity as a prerequisite for marriage, and the relative scarcity of positions available to unmarried women in the society which produced the text are all relevant considerations here. Where marriage is the primary avenue through which female prestige can be secured, and the loss of one's sexual purity can become an obstacle to marriage, it is not inconceivable that a woman would prefer to take advantage of the androcentric rationale which expresses itself in the Deuteronomic law and choose marriage over non-marriage. At any rate, the perspective from which the story is told seems to be based upon such logic.

Amnon, however, is not persuaded by Tamar's words. By contrasting her words with Amnon's response, we not only build up a picture of Tamar, we also build up a picture of Amnon. The effect is a negative one: Amnon is portrayed as cruel, manipulative, and one of the 'fools' or 'disgraceful men in Israel' (הנבלים בישראל). He sends her away, and uses one of his servants to do so.

Tamar's sorrow is vividly portrayed in v. 19, where she places ashes on her head, tears the robe she is wearing, and goes away crying out loud. Absalom sees her in this situation and deciphers the cause of her sorrow, for in v. 20 he asks Tamar whether Amnon has been with her. Tamar herself says nothing and, in fact, we do not hear from Tamar again. Absalom sends her away, suggesting that she not take the incident to heart. The last information we receive about her is given in v. 20, where we are told that she remained 'desolate' (שממה) in her brother's house. In light of the use of this word in Isa. 54.1, the description of Tamar may allude to her continued unmarried status (McCarter 1984: 326) and surely indicates the unhappy fate that was thought to await her.

Like the other women we have seen, Tamar is finally represented within a web of relations among male characters. Her rape is a functional event, but it occurs in a chain of events from which she quickly disappears. On the other hand, brief though her position as subject of speech and focalization may be, her words and anguish do offer a standpoint from which we can recognize that the text refrains from offering such a position to the other women we have seen, and to other women which we will examine below. The effect of focusing upon this position can be quite powerful, as Trible's reading of the story, for example, shows. Tamar's words, by their very contrast with the silence (or, to say the same thing negatively, lack of access to the position of speaking subject) which we find in the cases of the other women, help to disclose one of the issues which Bal has tried to underscore with her notion of focalization: the text, by choosing some points of view as relevant for inclusion and excluding others, constitutes a discourse which not only represents, but also inscribes, power relations.

Absalom's reappearance in v. 20 is quickly followed by David's reappearance in v. 21. David hears what has taken place and is angry.

His anger is qualified, in the manuscript tradition represented at Qumran and in the Septuagint (cf. McCarter 1984: 319), by the fact that he does not want to punish his son, whom he loves very much. The additional notation can be considered an explanation for a fact which the Masoretic Text simply shows us without explanation: angry though he may be, David does nothing to reprimand Abner or console Tamar.

The anthropological frame can help us to explore the possible consequences of David's inaction for the reader's evaluation of his character. Leaving aside for a moment the kinship relations between the male characters, an audience sharing the values associated with male honor and shame would almost surely have understood, and perhaps even expected, a response of *vengeance*. The rape of Tamar might have been interpreted not only as an affront to her, but also as an affront to the male kinsmen responsible for her sexual purity. In this case, those kinsmen would be her father and the brother with whom she is most closely associated, Absalom.

Here, however, the situation is made ambiguous by the fact that David is the father of each of the major players. While on the one hand he might have been expected to take vengeance against a man who raped his daughter, or to encourage his son to do so, on the other hand the subject of the rape is also his son and, moreover, his firstborn. David would seem to be *caught between* two imperatives of masculine honor which, in this situation, are at odds with one another: the imperative to avenge the honor of his family (as challenged through his daughter), and the imperative to honor the relations of kinship. The difficult situation in which David is placed here can be read in the light of YHWH's threat of judgment in the previous chapter. If David is placed between conflicting loyalties, YHWH can be, and generally has been, considered to have placed him there. As it turns out, it is Absalom rather than David (and probably in an intentional contrast with David) who responds to Amnon's treatment of Tamar.

The actions of David and Absalom can be usefully compared to the actions of Jacob and his sons after the rape of Dinah. Dinah's brothers respond to the treatment of their sister by killing the rapist (Shechem) and the men of his city and by taking their possessions (Gen. 34.25-29). Jacob, however, is displeased by this response and reprimands his sons (v. 30). His retort could be taken to mean that the 'challenge/response' dialectic, known to us from the anthropological literature on honor and shame, is *not* held in high esteem by the ideological subject of the biblical text. It is clear, after all, that Jacob denies the validity of the particular response of his sons, and specifically Simeon and Levi (cf. Gen. 49.5-7). Their response is a riposte to what they consider to be a challenge to their honor via the sexual purity of their sister (cf. Fewell and Gunn 1993: 84; Steinberg 1993: 110-11). In 34.31 Simeon and Levi retort, when reprimanded by their father, 'Will he treat our sister like a whore?' These words call to mind the words of the young male informant cited by Giovannini (1981: 408): 'Well, if we have a sister, Carlo and I will have to make sure no one calls her *puttana* [whore] or else our family will be laughed at'. Simeon and Levi seem to embody the more aggressive components of the ideology of honor and shame, in relation to the sexual purity of kinswomen. Their response is also congruent with that of Absalom: the sons (Absalom and Simeon/Levi) respond to the rapes of their sisters by seeking revenge, exactly as the anthropological literature would lead us to expect. Yet in both instances, the father of the raped woman apparently does not see this response as the most suitable way of handling the situation. Is it possible that we have to do here with a *rebuttal* of the protocols of honor/shame?

Upon closer examination, this does not appear likely. Dinah's rapist *does* wish to marry Dinah, and the specification of his love for her (Gen. 34.3) contrasts with the emotions and behavior of Amnon after the rape of Tamar. Shechem's attempt to marry Dinah proceeds by way of a negotiation with Dinah's kinsmen and a specific invitation to enter into a male alliance via the traffic in women ('give your daughters to us and take our daughters for yourselves', Gen. 34.9). This attitude coheres with the laws concerning rape that we have already seen. Moreover, Shechem and his father act in exactly the manner which *Tamar* recommends to Amnon: by effecting a marriage between the raped woman and the man who has raped her. If Jacob criticizes the actions of his sons, it is because they cut off a negotiating process which is considered proper. Amnon, by contrast, refuses to enter into this process from the beginning, so that Absalom's response to Amnon is not, in fact, a response to an identical set of circumstances. David's inaction, then, is not parallel to that of Jacob.

The events associated with Tamar's rape are only the first in a series of events that will progressively alienate David and Absalom from one another. This alienation, culminating in Absalom's rebellion against his father's sovereignty and, eventually, in his own death, can thus be seen as the outcome of the sexual action perpetrated by Amnon in ch. 13.

Yet once again, the important narrative role assigned to the sexual action must be evaluated within its overall context. So far as David is concerned, it is the death of Amnon rather than the rape of Tamar which has continuing significance. At the end of ch. 13, Amnon's death is specifically referred to once again, and the dialogue with the woman of Tekoa clearly deals with the fratricide. Tamar, by contrast, is not mentioned. Her importance within the overall narrative is related to her status as point of conflict between male characters. Although Absalom does name one of his daughters Tamar, and so can be interpreted as being concerned about his sister, neither David nor the narrator seem interested in her character once the rape and its immediate aftermath have passed.

The role of the rape of Tamar within the larger narrative depends upon the fact that Absalom can interpret Amnon's action as a message, indeed, a message against him:

Amnon >> Tamar >> Absalom

The message, interpreted from Absalom's end, is not simply one of desire, although desire clearly plays a role in ch. 13, but rather one of honor. Amnon is considered to have challenged, via the sexual purity of Tamar, the honor of Absalom. Absalom, however, responds according to the protocols of a certain configuration of manhood. We can even say that Absalom tries to show Amnon, and perhaps David, who the 'better man' is. As we shall now see, this is not the last instance in which Absalom and his masculinity play an important narrative role.

2 Samuel 16.20-23

As was the case in 2 Samuel 3, a scene which we can call 'sexual' appears in 2 Samuel 16 in the midst of a storyline focused upon the politics of kingship: male characters are struggling with one another for the throne of Israel. There are other similarities between the two stories as well, and scholars have frequently interpreted the stories as manifestations of a similar social ideology. Like Abner's actions in 2 Samuel 3, the actions taken by Absalom in 2 Samuel 16 are explained by reference to a reconstructed 'custom' about monarchical legitimacy and the wives or concubines of a previous ruler.

There are also differences between the two texts, however, and these differences need to be accounted for in a plausible interpretation. Absalom, unlike Abner, is specifically represented as seeking Israel's throne. His royal ambitions are not in doubt, and so a certain amount of ambiguity which is present in 2 Samuel 3 is absent from 2 Samuel 16. After Absalom goes to Hebron to make himself king, David and his officials flee Jerusalem, apparently afraid that Absalom will attack the city. The narrator recounts the departure of David and his followers, but also notes that ten of David's concubines remained in Jerusalem to take care of the house (2 Sam. 15.16).

These concubines are not mentioned again until after Absalom and his followers have arrived in Jerusalem (2 Sam. 16.15). Absalom asks Ahithophel, a former counselor of David, for advice about what ought to be done. Ahithophel instructs Absalom to have sexual relations with (literally 'go in to', בוֹא) the concubines, so that 'all Israel will hear that you have become odious (כִּי־נִבְאַשְׁתָּ)' to David and 'the hands of all who are with you will be strengthened' (16.21). A tent is placed on the roof, and 'Absalom went in to the concubines of his father (וַיָּבֹא אַבְשָׁלוֹם אֶל־פִּלַגְשֵׁי אָבִיו) in front of all Israel' (16.22). The public nature of the sexual contact is indicated clearly in the text, as is the relationship between the concubines and Absalom's father.

On one level, Absalom's action is clearly a fulfillment of YHWH's threat to David, in 2 Sam. 12.11, to take David's women and give them to David's neighbor, who will lie with them in front of Israel. However, a motivation for Absalom's action is also supplied by Ahithophel in the text. This motivation has two dimensions. First, by having sexual relations with the concubines of David, Absalom will 'become odious' to his father, as all Israel will hear. Secondly, those who support Absalom will be encouraged and strengthened in their task when they hear what Absalom has done. It is possible that this second motivation is understood to be accomplished by the first: Absalom's supporters are heartened by the fact that he has 'made himself odious' to his father. But what does this mean?

The term in v. 21 which is generally translated 'become odious' (נִבְאַשְׁתָּ) refers literally to having a bad smell. The root (בָּאַשׁ) appears only three times in one of its *niphal* forms. However, there is an important occurrence elsewhere in 2 Samuel where another subject 'becomes odious' to David. In 2 Sam. 10.6 the Ammonites see that they have 'become odious' or 'been a stink' (נִבְאֲשׁוּ) to David when the Ammonite king shaves the beards and cuts the skirts of David's emissaries. The actions taken toward these men seem to cause shame, for the men are sent by David to Jericho where they will remain until their beards grow out.

This notation indicates that the removal of the men's beards is as much a cause of shame as is their nakedness. When the Ammonites see that, by these actions, they have 'become a stink' to David, they proceed to make preparations for battle. Their actions lead to an intensification of conflict.

In 2 Samuel 16, then, Ahithophel seems to be saying that Absalom's actions will produce an effect which is in some sense parallel to the actions of the Ammonites in 2 Samuel 10. However, Ahithophel's words to Absalom are not always referred to when scholars account for Absalom's actions. Instead, the case in 2 Samuel 16 is often conflated with the stories in 2 Samuel 3 and 1 Kings 2 as justification for the reconstructed custom of harem possession as a means of legitimizing one's own claim to the throne. I have already suggested that this explanation, nowhere stated in the text, is not, at least as it is generally formulated, a sufficient interpretation of the ideological complex under-lying 2 Samuel 3. In 2 Samuel 16, the hypothesis meets the additional obstacle that it plays no specific role in Ahithophel's account of the meanings involved. He gives not so much as a hint that Absalom's action is, for example, 'a state act equivalent to a declaration that the previous king is dead' (Hertzberg 1964: 350). On the contrary, the king in question is explicitly the first intended recipient of the message which Absalom's actions will send. Absalom wishes to produce a negative effect, signified by the verb already referred to, on his father.

The possible significance of Absalom's action appears in a different light when the text is placed within an anthropological frame. Absalom's sexual activity with his father's concubines can be read as an attempt to attack David's gender-based prestige, rather than as a simple declaration that David is no longer king. By having sexual relations with the ten concubines of David, Absalom has demonstrated David's inability to fulfill a crucial part of a culturally inscribed view of masculinity. As all Israel can see, David has been unable to maintain control over sexual access to the women of his house, and so has failed with regard to what is, in many cultures, a critical criterion for the assessment of manhood.

This demonstration has intended consequences for both Absalom and David. Absalom has attempted to increase his own prestige by showing his ability to take what David ought to be, but is not, able to control. However, it is not simply David's ability to control that has been placed in question. David's social masculinity has also been challenged. The effects upon David's reputation can be read in terms of Gilmore's suggestion that the man who becomes a victim, through the women associated with him, of another man's sexual assertiveness has been symbolically feminized (Gilmore 1987a: 11). Lacking a crucial element of a cultural definition of masculinity, he falls perilously close to femininity. He is symbolically emasculated.

It is here that the linguistic intertextual link with 2 Samuel 10 becomes significant. Both the Ammonites and Absalom 'become odious' to David. I want to suggest that, in both instances, this effect is achieved in part by attacking the symbolic masculinity, and by extension the gender-based prestige, of the king. The Ammonites cut the skirts and the beards of David's messengers. It seems to be generally understood that the nakedness of these men produces shame, but the significance, in certain cultures, of the removal of the beards may be unclear to modern Anglo-American readers. However, facial hair, and indeed body hair in general, is often a potent gender signifier. Maud Gleason has pointed out, for example, that such ancient authors as Aristotle, Epictetus, Musonius and Clement of Alexandria seem to have interpreted a profusion of body hair as a sign of virility and a lack of body hair as a sign of effeminacy. This interpretation was apparently based upon the belief of some ancient writers that a 'man's natural hair was the product of the same abundance of inner heat that concocted his sperm' (Gleason 1990: 400-401). Consequently, depilation was often seen as an attempt to remove the natural marks of masculinity from one's body. Similar connotations still occur in ethnographic accounts of more recent societies. Bourdieu can quote his informants as saying, 'I've got a moustache too', when they want to assert the equivalence of their honor with that of other men. Bourdieu explains that facial hair is considered 'a symbol of virility', and that the removal of the beard by another man stands metaphorically for social humiliation (Bourdieu 1979: 100; cf. Campbell 1964: 280; Laqueur 1990: 101).

One can compare the biblical case of Samson. Samson's long hair is attributed in Judg. 13.5 to his status as a Nazirite, but the regulations pertaining to Nazirites in Numbers 6 do not give a clear explanation for the fact that Nazirites were to refrain from cutting their hair. The narrative in Judges, however, clearly links Samson's extraordinary strength to the length of his hair. When Delilah cuts Samson's hair his strength disappears, though this strength returns miraculously after his hair is explicitly noted to have grown again (16.22). Samson is, moreover, characterized in terms of his relations with women and so, possibly, in terms of his virility (one commentator refers to 'his powerful libido' [Leith 1993: 673]), and it is therefore not altogether surprising that interpreters have occasionally seen in the cutting of Samson's hair a sort of 'symbolic castration' (see, for example, Exum 1993: 79).

So far as 2 Samuel 10 is concerned, McCarter has already suggested with respect to the removal of the beards of David's messengers that such an act 'symbolically deprives a man of his masculinity'. Hence, David's messengers, too, are subjected to 'symbolic castration' (McCarter 1984: 270). McCarter's choice of words here is exactly right. The Ammonites deprive David's emissaries of one of the signals by which one's manhood is publicly affirmed. The treatment of the messengers may be an insult as well to the one from whom the messengers came, and whose representatives they are. What kind of king, an ancient audience might well ask, allows his subjects to be treated in such a manner? The act is a sort of challenge, for which David's own masculine honor requires a response.

If the actions of the Ammonites constitute a symbolic emasculation, such may also be the case with the actions of Absalom. Both the Ammonites and, according to Ahithophel, Absalom can produce the same effect: make themselves a stench to David. To restate this effect in the discourse of anthropology, we might say that the Ammonites and Absalom both attempt to shame David. While the Ammonites attack David's prestige by attacking his representatives, Absalom attacks David's prestige by attacking his women. The specific connotations of the two cases are not identical, but the effect (signified by the use of the same language) and the process ('symbolic castration') of these cases overlap significantly.

While the Ammonites focus upon the gender connotations of body hair, Absalom focuses upon the gender connotations of the attitude taken toward the sexuality of the women of one's household. The concubines become a means with which Absalom can attack David's masculinity. If David were 'good at being a man', the audience might assume, he would not have left himself open to this sort of attack. A properly vigilant attitude on his part toward the concubines would have prevented such an event from taking place. There are, as Ahithophel implies, two effects to be achieved here: David has been shamed in his own eyes, but his prestige in the eyes of other men has also been diminished, even as Absalom's has increased. The concubines themselves thus become the 'conduit of a relationship' (Rubin 1975): a relation on the one hand between David and Absalom, and a relation on the other hand between Absalom and the men who support him, who will, it is hoped, be sufficiently impressed with Absalom's manhood to fight even harder for his cause.

The demonstration of Absalom's masculinity in terms of cultural signifiers of manhood seems to be an issue elsewhere in the texts. Absalom has already responded to the rape of his sister by killing the rapist. As I have suggested above, it is Absalom's vengeance, rather than David's inaction, that is most consistent with the norms of masculine honor as these norms are laid out in the anthropological literature, and this contrast sets the stage for the conflicts which follow.

Moreover, the notation of Absalom's own profusion of hair (2 Sam. 14.26) may be more than simply a statement about his good looks, although his good looks, too, are specified (v. 25) and, indeed, seem to have been themselves an important characteristic of potential kings (cf., for example, 1 Sam. 9.2; 16.12; 1 Kgs 1.6). In the light of the symbolic connotations of body hair mentioned above, it is possible that Absalom's thick hair may also hint at his virility, and it is therefore ironic that this feature turns out to be connected to his undoing. The narrator is careful to tell us that Absalom had to cut his hair each year because it grew so thick and became heavy. The explanation is quickly followed by an account of the birth of Absalom's sons and a daughter (2 Sam. 14.27). Although this note conflicts with information given elsewhere (2 Sam. 18.18) which indicates that Absalom had no sons, within the context of ch. 14 the information about sons and a daughter can be seen as a logical culmination of the preceding verses. The signification of Absalom's potency is complete, inasmuch as the ability to sire children is also an important cultural signifier of successful manhood (cf. Gilmore 1990: 41-42). Absalom is characterized here as the pinnacle of masculinity.

Furthermore, the texts which recount Absalom's rebellion clearly narrate a process by which Absalom attempts to show himself to be potentially a better king than David, precisely because his actions are more successful than those of his father. In addition to gathering horses, chariots, and soldiers, Absalom stands near the gate of the city and claims that his own distribution of justice would be superior to that of his father (2 Sam. 15.1-4). This claim is specifically an attempt to win over the hearts of the people by increasing his own worth in their eyes, but the attempt also has an apparent competitive quality: Absalom is not only good, he is superior to his father the king.

Thus, 2 Samuel contains a number of facts about Absalom which can be seen as playing upon conventional sources of prestige. Some of these elements are related to traditional ideas about the duties of a king, such as the ability to dispense justice, but others have a more specific relation to gender-specific prestige: the profusion of hair, the ability to sire children, and good looks. In at least some of these instances, Absalom claims not only to possess a source of prestige, but to possess it in greater quantity than his father.

This is the context in which Absalom's possession of David's concubines ought to be seen. Absalom is playing publicly to a particular element of masculine prestige, the ability to control access to the women of one's household. Like the references to body hair, the production of children, and so forth, this element has a gender-specific quality to it: it is not just a quality of kings, but of prestigious men in general, of which the king must certainly be one. At the same time, like the reference to the dispensation of justice, Absalom demonstrates his own abilities in this particular area in a way that compares them to those of his father. Absalom is, to utilize Herzfeld's terminology once again, *better* at being a man than David—and therefore better at being a king. Such, at any rate, is the claim which he wishes to make.

In this case, of course, the man whose honor and power he challenges is his own father. Since a man's honor is tied up with the honor of his family, and since, moreover, a certain attitude of respect toward one's father might itself be a criterion for honor (and is certainly a criterion for respect elsewhere in the Hebrew Bible), Absalom's actions may have an effect which is quite different from that which he intends, and which Ahithophel suggests. In the end, his claim to be an honorable man might be undermined, not because he has chosen the realm of sexual practice to demonstrate his claim, but because the man over against whom he demonstrates his claim is his own father.

Indeed, an interesting parallel in the book of Genesis forces us to consider this possibility. In Gen. 35.22 there is a brief notice that Reuben had sexual intercourse with the concubine of his father Jacob. This sexual action becomes a motivation in 49.4 for some sort of loss of status on the part of the tribe of Reuben. While the story of Reuben is not identical to that in 2 Samuel 16, the evaluation of Reuben's conduct does perhaps indicate that in spite of Ahithophel's words, Absalom's actions might not have unambiguously positive effects on his honor. Regardless of the impact of the act on Absalom's reputation, however, David's honor is clearly under attack.

In any event, it is not necessary to link this story too closely to a general 'custom' or 'state act' about monarchical legitimacy and the wives and concubines of a former king. Such a link would construe the women as property of sorts which a new king inherits along with the throne. This view clearly lies behind Hertzberg's interpretation, noted above, that Absalom has in effect declared David to be dead by seizing his property. Much more important is the competitive element involved in the relative ability of two living men to control sexual access to particular women. This site of conflict is often an important locus for the social determination of male prestige, and there is little reason to believe that kings and potential kings would be any less subject to gender-specific norms of social worth than other persons.

Indeed, the texts of Samuel presuppose at numerous points that a legitimate king is not simply the son of a previous king, but one who is able to demonstrate qualities deemed positive. When YHWH chooses as king someone who bears these qualities within himself, this is the result of a projection by a particular culture of their own social views about prestige, gender, and power onto their deity. To be sure, the results are never straightforward: persons contain within themselves the sources of prestige to varying degrees, and these sources can conflict with one another, so that a person who possesses certain admirable qualities in sufficient quantity may nevertheless lack others. It is precisely the tension and competition involved in this process which a successful story about the struggle for the throne is able to play upon, a story, for example, like that of Absalom and David, both of whom seem to be viewed both positively and negatively at various points in the narrative.

Throughout the text which recounts this story, however, the women who play a role in the process are seen only briefly. The concubines constitute a site for the conflict between father and son, but they never obtain the position of narrative subject. There is little reason to consider that women in such a situation would have been willing participants. The only other reference to these women comes in ch. 20 when, after David's return to Jerusalem, he refuses to go in to them and has them put away until, living like widows (20.3), they eventually die. It is possible to see here a parallel to the desolation of Tamar, who suffered a similar fate after her own rape. If the anguish of these women is in any way similar to that expressed by Tamar, however, it has been silenced entirely by the text. Their relations with men (including, ironically, the man who killed his brother after the rape of Tamar) seem to have interested the narrator only to the degree that these relations impact relations between men. Once again, heterosexual bonds and homosocial bonds become, within the narrative discourse, impossible to disentangle.

1 Kings 2

A discussion of 1 Kings 2 in a study of narratives that utilize sexual scenes might seem unnecessary, since no sexual acts are actually recounted here. The only clear reference to sexual activity comes in 1 Kgs 1.4, where we are told that the aging king David did *not* have sexual relations with Abishag, the young woman who had been brought to the king to keep him warm. This notation of a *lack* of sexual subjectivity on David's part can itself be seen as a means of characterizing the king. In a context where one's sexual practice influences the perception of one's manhood, David is unable to demonstrate his virility. Here we may have to do with a cultural perception of a lack of sexual vigor thought to be characteristic of old age (cf. Gen. 18.12).

In ch. 2, after his initial attempt to inherit David's throne has been thwarted, Adonijah comes to Bathsheba with a request. Adonijah wants Bathsheba to persuade Solomon to give Abishag to him as his wife (2.17). This request is important for the present study because it is often cited together with 2 Samuel 3 and 2 Samuel 16 as evidence for the hypothetical custom concerning monarchical legitimacy and the wives and concubines of a previous king. Thus, the interpretation of this story conceivably impacts the plausibility which one grants to the interpretation of the other two stories. The three stories are, however, less similar than commentators have sometimes implied.

It is clear that Adonijah, like Absalom but unlike Abner, desires the throne of Israel. Throughout ch. 1, the narrator recounts in detail the process by which Adonijah consolidates his support as a claimant for the throne. Several details of this process are reminiscent of Absalom's earlier attempt to secure the throne of Israel, and so we have hints about some of the criteria by which one attempted to establish monarchical legitimacy. We are told that Adonijah gathers chariots and soldiers (1.5), that he was 'handsome' (1.6), that he was the next eldest son after Absalom (1.6), that he acquired some powerful supporters among Israel's elite (1.7), and that he organized a sacrificial feast to which a portion of Israel's nobility, excluding the supporters of Solomon, were invited (1.9-10). All of this information is presented as part of the process by which

Adonijah attempts to maneuver to succeed his father as Israel's king.

If it is true, as Levenson and Halpern, for example, suggest, that 'a custom apparently well-founded in Israel' existed whereby 'through the carnal knowledge of a suzerain's harem a man could lay claim to suzerainty himself' (Levenson and Halpern 1980: 508), we might expect some manifestation of this custom to appear at that stage in the plot where Adonijah is most vigorously attempting to lay such a claim. In other words, Adonijah's attempt to secure Abishag as his wife would most logically appear along with the other steps which he takes to increase the likelihood of his own succession. In the story, however, Adonijah's request for Abishag only appears *after* Adonijah's supporters have abandoned him (1.49) and, it having become clear that Solomon will sit upon the throne, Adonijah has done obeisance to his brother (1.53). This seems a most unlikely time to initiate a process which might call to mind a 'well-founded custom' about monarchical legitimacy. Thus, it is necessary to consider whether another plausible account of the significance of Adonijah's request and Solomon's reply might be constructed.

The text segment that is most crucial for interpreting the significance of Adonijah's request is Solomon's response to his mother. Bathsheba, following Adonijah's suggestion, approaches her son and asks that Abishag be given to Adonijah. Solomon, who has already stated that he will not refuse his mother's request, nevertheless changes his mind immediately:

> But King Solomon answered his mother, 'And why are you requesting Abishag the Shunammite for Adonijah? Request for him the kingdom, because he is my older brother! For him and for Abiathar the priest and for Joab the son of Zeruiah!' And King Solomon swore by YHWH, 'Thus may God do to me and more, because Adonijah did this thing at the risk of his life. And now, as YHWH lives who established me and put me on the throne of David my father, and who made me a house just as he said, today Adonijah will die!' (2.22-24)

Clearly, some sort of link is made here between Adonijah's request for Abishag and the possibility that Adonijah might sit upon the throne ('You might as well ask for him the kingdom as well!'). The normal manner of handling this text is to find within Solomon's response an accusation that Adonijah has still further ambitions for the throne, ambitions which Adonijah intends to support by marrying a woman associated with his father. Since, as one commentator puts it, the 'appropriation of the harem of the late king' can constitute 'an indirect claim to the throne', Solomon seizes, perhaps 'too eagerly', upon these connotations to use them as a 'pretext' for eliminating Adonijah (Gray 1963: 103).

Once again, however, we have a text which is extremely ambiguous, and for which a number of interpretations can be postulated. The ambiguities involved are apparent even in Gray's comments, just quoted, since he recognizes that any actual plotting on Adonijah's part is, at this point in the story, far from clear. Indeed, Adonijah admits explicitly to Bathsheba that YHWH himself has given the throne to his younger brother Solomon (2.15). Moreover, Adonijah, by acknowledging Solomon's right to arbitrate in the matter of sexual access to Abishag, has already granted to Solomon a position of relative power over against any men who might wish to marry her, including Adonijah himself. Yet Solomon clearly views Adonijah's request with suspicion and anger, so much so that he decides to have his brother put to death. The question that remains, then, and that impacts my interpretation of these stories, is that of the ideological complex underlying Solomon's angry response. What significance might conceivably be attributed to Adonijah's request such that Solomon was able to use it as justification for Adonijah's death? Would the acquisition of one of the concubines of the former king in and of itself be sufficient evidence for concluding that Adonijah's intentions are dubious? Can the mode of acquisition of women which is actually at stake in this particular story be compared unproblematically to the mode of acquisition which we have already seen in 2 Samuel 3 and 2 Samuel 16?

In order to answer these questions, it needs to be pointed out that we are not dealing here, as we were in 2 Samuel 3 and 2 Samuel 16, with sexual contact outside of marriage. On the contrary, we are dealing with a request for marriage, a rather different affair. Hence, if we are to interpret this text intertextually, it is not clear that 2 Samuel 3 and 2 Samuel 16 are the texts with which 1 Kings 2 might most logically be compared. We need to consider other stories in which an explicit request for marriage is at stake. There is, for example, the case of David and his request for remarriage with Michal, a request that does seem to be linked to the legitimacy of his kingship in some way. This marriage was obtained precisely through negotiations with another man whose power to give Michal was assumed. Hence, the negotiating process presupposes the institution of a relation between the two parties to the negotiation: David and the man who has it within his power to give Michal in marriage (cf. 2. Sam 3.12-16).

We can recall, in the light of Rubin's reading of Lévi-Strauss, that marriage alliances comprise one of the most significant nodes in the network of social relations constituted by the 'traffic in women': the woman who becomes a wife serves as the 'conduit of a relationship' between the husband and her male kinsman. It seems to follow that a man who acquires as wife one of the women associated with a king or other person of high status, and who does so by way of negotiation, forges thereby a relation of some positive sort with the other (generally male) person.

Now it is probably the case that it is the ability to secure the alliance with a prominent person that enhances the prestige, in the eyes of other men, of the otherwise subordinate partner to this deal. Let us take the case of David once again. If, by marriage to Michal, David was able to increase the positive evaluation of his status and social position, this effect was the result of the social link which was consequently understood to exist between David and a house of high social reputation, that is, the ruling house of Saul. This change in David's own status does perhaps increase his perceived suitability for the role of king, but not because Michal carries within herself some sort of inherent value such that marrying her will assure one's claim upon the throne. Rather, an increase in David's prestige comes about because of the fact that a man of higher social standing has publicly considered David worthy of marrying one of his daughters. As David himself exclaims at one point, who is he that he should become the king's son-in-law (1 Sam. 18.18)? The question shows that it is the association established with a king of Israel which enhances David's social reputation. Far from challenging Saul's own prestige, however, this sort of negotiation *presupposes* and hence affirms it.

At the same time, the marriage alliance alone would by no means have assured David's succession to the throne of Israel. After all, Saul's daughter Merab, first offered to David by her father, was finally given instead to Adriel the Meholathite (1 Sam. 18.19), and Michal herself was given to Paltiel the son of Laish after the conflict between Saul and David became acute (1 Sam. 25.44). Yet so far as we can tell, neither of these two men was ever considered a contender for the throne. It is thus not so much the marriage alliance in isolation, but rather the way in which a marriage alliance can be capitalized upon together with other variables, that explains the link between marriage alliances and royal legitimacy. The relation which one is able to establish between one's own person and the men of the royal house by way of the marriage alliance enhances one's prestige, and thereby puts one in a position in which one is better able to maneuver for the throne by deploying many different strategies for the acquisition of power. David's marriage with Michal seems to have been but one of a bundle of features on the basis of which David came to be seen as a legitimate king.

To return to the case of Adonijah and Solomon, Adonijah seems to have been removed from consideration as a claimant to the throne, and might suffer from the shame of having been usurped by his younger brother. The attempt to secure Abishag as his wife can be interpreted as an initial attempt at rehabilitating his social reputation. This rehabilitation could *possibly* be seen as a first step on the way to conspiring yet again for the throne, and this possibility may be one upon which Solomon seizes in order to rid himself of his brother. Yet it is not clear that this motivation must have been automatically attributed to Adonijah's request, since he may simply have been trying to improve his lot. Having fallen in terms of his own social standing, Adonijah hopes to increase his reputation by securing a more positive relationship with his brother Solomon. The sign with which he hopes to see such an improved relationship confirmed is an agreement that he shall be allowed to marry one of the women whom Solomon now has the power to give and take. Such an agreement would not so much challenge as presuppose Solomon's powerful position.

The vehemence of Solomon's angry response may be due to the manner in which Adonijah attempts to obtain Abishag. Adonijah does not approach Solomon directly with his request, which would have been the clearest way of acknowledging Solomon's status relative to that of Adonijah. Rather, he tries in an indirect way to influence Solomon by manipulating the king's mother. Instead of risking the possibility that Solomon has no desire to grant a request that will in any way increase Adonijah's status, Adonijah attempts to reach the same goal by utilizing Bathsheba and her influence over the king.

Thus, it is Bathsheba rather than Abishag who has by far the more important narrative position within the first two chapters of 1 Kings. If we assume a context in which men are understood to manipulate their relations with women in order to achieve certain goals in the realm of their relations with men, as I have argued, then the particular relations at work in any situation must be considered in their specificity. Here, Adonijah does not only work to obtain a more prominent position by securing a marriage alliance with a woman of the royal household. He also uses another woman of the royal household, the queen mother, as a tool for achieving his ends. This manipulation of the king's mother by Adonijah for his own ends should be taken into account in any evaluation of Solomon's subsequent actions.

The mother–son relationship is an enormously complex and potent symbol in many different cultures (see, for instance, Gilmore 1987a; Campbell 1964: 164-66). To be sure, the specific content of this symbol, as well as the relationship itself and the role of a 'mother' in general, is much more variable than has often been assumed (cf. Moore 1988: 25-30). It should not be surprising, however, if the symbolic dimensions of this relation were capitalized upon in narratives from ancient societies.

Indeed, within the bounds of the Hebrew Bible, we know that narrative effects were sometimes achieved by playing upon this relationship. Thus, Jephthah, the son of a prostitute, is driven away by his brothers on account of his mother's identity (Judg. 11). When Saul becomes angry with his son, Jonathan, over the relationship which has developed between Jonathan and David, he responds by insulting Jonathan's mother while apparently claiming simultaneously that Jonathan's actions have themselves brought shame upon his mother (1 Sam. 20.30). Interestingly, the language which Saul utilizes itself has sexual overtones, since he refers to the 'nakedness' of Jonathan's mother. The ancestral narratives, and notably the narratives about Rebekah and Jacob, also play upon the mother-son relationship in intriguing ways.

In light of these examples of a rhetorical utilization of the mother–son relationship, it seems wise to insist that, when such a relationship appears in a biblical text, it ought to be assessed carefully for its possible symbolic and ideological significance rather than subordinated to another male–female relation (in this case, that between Abishag and the father of the two brothers). One must question whether interpretations which assess Solomon's anger almost solely in terms of the status of Abishag, while paying little attention to the status of Bathsheba, have actually grasped the dynamics of the story. Here it is Solomon's mother who becomes the 'conduit of a relationship' between two men struggling for power.

The fact that Adonijah feels compelled to achieve his goals by speaking to Bathsheba seems to imply that a straightforward request to Solomon might not have been successful. Solomon would seem to have had no desire to enhance, in any manner whatsoever, the prestige of the man who has tried to secure the throne in his place. Thus, Adonijah's actions are an attempt to circumvent Solomon's direct wishes by manipulating one of the persons closest to him, his mother. It may be this attempt at manipulation that particularly angers Solomon, and leads to his caustic response about giving Adonijah the throne as well. Solomon is able to see through Adonijah's trick, in what is perhaps the first of a number of instances in which Solomon's legendary 'wisdom' is displayed in narrative form.

This is not the first time that Bathsheba figures in the plot as the object of male schemes. Her son sits upon the throne in part because Nathan was able to use Bathsheba to convince David to put an end to any uncertainty about his successor. As we have already seen, she functions in the story of David and Uriah almost entirely as an object, responding to David's words and actions. Thus, Bathsheba's primary narrative subject-position is as the object of another man's plots. It is easy to criticize and raise questions about the gender implications of a statement such as that of Whybray, who refers to 'a thoroughly credible picture of Bathsheba as a good-natured, rather stupid woman who was a natural prey both to more passionate and to cleverer men' (Whybray 1968: 40). However, it needs to be recognized that a reading such as Whybray's is at least partially the effect of certain narrative structures, and of the subject positions allotted (or not allotted) to particular gendered characters within those structures.

We can see here the possible outline of another sort of narrative convention, apart from an explicitly sexual one, in which men manipulate male–female relations to obtain certain effects of power and prestige. It is this relation between Solomon and Adonijah *via Bathsheba*, however, and not by way of Abishag, that is the dominant element here. This relation deserves a more extended examination in its own right, as one of a possible series of texts which might illuminate the ideological associations of 'mother' in ancient Israelite literature (cf. Exum 1993: 94-147; Fuchs 1985). However, such an examination falls outside of the scope of my project. Hence, though the story fits into the much larger context of biblical stories in which the exchange of women figures in the plot, the specifically *sexual* elements present in the other texts that I have examined are much less important (if they are present at all) here. The case of Abishag is thus not as similar to the other instances of disputed concubines as a conflation of the various cases implies, and should be more carefully differentiated from them in the future.

Chapter 5

CONCLUSIONS

Sex, Honor, and Power in the Deuteronomistic History

In spite of the attention that has been given to sexual matters in the preceding pages, it would be wrong to suggest that the narratives of the Deuteronomistic History are in some way fascinated with sexual relations. At no point, for example, have we seen detailed descriptions of sexual contact. On the contrary, at least one of the stories (2 Sam. 3.6-11), though structured in relation to an instance of sexual contact, does not directly narrate the sexual act at all but reveals it instead during a later discourse of one of the characters. Sexual activity exists as part of the pre-text of the Deuteronomistic History. Its existence is taken for granted by the narrative, just as the existence of priests, sacrifices, wars, marriages, kinship relations, and other significant and insignificant aspects of reality are assumed and utilized in the storytelling process.

Yet if the Deuteronomistic History does not sensationalize sexual practice, neither does it ignore the complex situations which sexual matters could sometimes generate. In the stories that we have seen, sexual contact of one sort or another has produced anger, revenge, shame, sorrow, deceit, and death. This is the first and perhaps the most important fact to recognize about sex and the Deuteronomistic History: sexual activity seems to be utilized in these narratives because of the results which it is considered capable of producing, and not because the realm of 'the sexual' per se is considered to be particularly interesting in either a positive or a negative sense.

Indeed, it seems doubtful that we can speak here of a 'realm' of the sexual at all. The sexual events that occur in the Deuteronomistic History are all integrated into larger narrative trajectories and cannot finally be separated from the political and religious events which surround them. Biblical scholars have sometimes been fond of saying that the Hebrew Bible knows nothing of a distinct religious realm, separate from the social and historical realities in which human beings live. If the Deuteronomistic History is to be taken as evidence, it is not certain that biblical scholars will be able to make use of any notion of a private sexual realm, either, at least for the purposes of textual interpretation. That sexual activity usually took place in private settings in Israel, with absolutely no impact whatsoever upon the course of history, is of course not being disputed here. The point is, instead, that the Deuteronomistic History does not seem to be interested in such matters, but rather in the sorts of situations that could arise under certain conditions as the result of a sexual event which became known to a wider audience.

Now it is clear that the circumstances surrounding sexual activity in the stories that have been examined are not identical to one another. Each of the stories has its own dynamic, its own constellation of characters, events, and results. It would certainly be wrong to conflate the stories simplistically and without regard for these differences, a fact which I have emphasized by suggesting that the story in 1 Kings 2 may have fewer points of contact with the other stories than has sometimes been assumed.

Yet a narratological analysis, proceeding by way of the question of the narrative subject, reveals a number of similarities between most of the otherwise disparate texts. For example, all of the sexual acts are related in some way to conflicts between male characters. Moreover, all of the sexual events in the texts that we have examined here are narrated as having been initiated by men. Male actors are sexual subjects. When the female characters act, they act in response to male characters. Some of the women are not represented as having acted at all. Only Tamar speaks, and her words constitute an attempt to prevent Amnon's actions. Tamar is also the only female character for which the narrative supplies anything like a perspective or opinion about the sexual events themselves.

So far as the structure of the narrative is concerned, then, there is little or no interest expressed in these particular women *as active initiators of sexual activity*. Apart from the case of Tamar, there is also little interest expressed in the possibility that the women may have tried to resist or fight off the sexual actions, some of which are extraordinarily violent. Even Tamar, whose anguish is exceptional inasmuch as it is the only female focalization of any sort of sexual contact in these narratives, disappears from sight after her brother Absalom sends her away. The text seems almost entirely uninterested in the possible points of view of the women involved. A narratological analysis indicates that the chief interest of the narratives under consideration lies in the actions of male characters, in the opinions of these male characters about the events that take place, and in the ways in which the events produce or fail to produce certain responses from other male characters.

In making this point, I wish to stress that I am not simply pointing out once again the male bias of the biblical texts, although an underscoring of that point, already made by others, is certainly one of the effects of the analysis. Rather, there is also a more specific point here. It has to do not only with the relative power allotted in the narrative to characters on the basis of their gender, although that has indeed been stressed. It has to do, in addition, with *a certain view of sexual activity, a certain cluster of interests and questions which surround sexual activity when it is represented in the biblical texts*. These interests have to do almost exclusively with male characters, in spite of the fact that, in sexual activity more so than in many other matters, female characters are, in the biblical texts, almost always involved. Sexual activity seems to concern the narrator almost entirely because of *its possible consequences for relationships between men*, and so becomes, within the narrative discourse of the Deuteronomistic History, a primarily homosocial affair. Other male characters are, so to speak, the initial audience of the sexual events that take place. It is first of all these other male characters who are represented as attributing meaning to sexual contact, and their semiotic activity mediates our own. If we wish to understand the possible meanings of the texts, we must first understand the possible meanings of the sexual acts for the characters who interact with one another in the story.

It is at this point that an anthropological framework assists us. An anthropological interpretation, resting necessarily upon a certain amount of comparative argumentation, cannot claim any final certainty or exclusive validity, as critics of comparativism never tire of pointing out. It is an admittedly interpretive enterprise, the validity of which rests upon the plausibility and persuasiveness of particular instances of reading. However, I have tried to show that a particular complex of anthropological information is able to shed light upon texts that are in many ways obscure and that seem to conflict with many of our own 'common sense' assumptions about the significance of sexual activity. The use of anthropology does not result in a more 'scientific' reading, although some critics utilizing the social sciences have implied as much; nor can it eliminate our subjective biases as readers, since social-scientific theories generally function as reading frames which enable us to generate hypotheses about the possible meanings and symbolic associations of a text. However, an anthropological framework does help us to articulate an interpretation of those texts that include particular types of sexual contact, and to do so in a way which at least attempts to avoid the impulse to universalize our own assumptions about sex and gender. Although an anthropological frame cannot eliminate our own biases with regard to the texts and the subject matter, it can help to relativize both our biases and the biases of the texts.

In light of the anthropological frame articulated in Chapter 2 and as part of an attempt to make sense of the results of a narratological analysis, we can suggest that all of these texts capitalize upon the potential for sexual acts to impact the honor, power, and prestige of men. This potential, known to us especially (but not exclusively) from the anthropological literature on the Mediterranean basin and parts of the Middle East, seems to manifest itself in several different ways in these texts. In some instances (such as Judg. 19; 2 Sam. 16) we apparently have a deliberate attempt by some men to shame other men, and to do so in a sexual manner. In other instances (such as 2 Sam. 3; 13) there does not seem to be a deliberate attempt to challenge the honor of another man, but one man who finds out about a sexual contact is apparently compelled, probably as a point of honor, to respond to the transgression of another man upon what is considered to be his symbolic territory, namely, the right to determine sexual access to a woman. The case of David, Bathsheba, and Uriah is perhaps the most complicated case of all, but can be seen as a permutation of the same ideological complex. In this instance, however, it is David's inability to negotiate among the norms of masculine honor and power, in their relation to sexual contact, which is illustrated by the narrative course of events. Sexual misconduct per se, apart from what is seen as the abuse of power by one male against another, does not seem to be a primary concern in the text, and is certainly not the overriding concern which later readers of 2 Samuel 11–12 have often imagined.

All of this has been discussed above. In the comments that follow, several additional matters will be mentioned which deserve further analysis in light of the issues discussed here. These comments are intended primarily as suggestions for future research, and not as definitive conclusions.

Sex in the Deuteronomistic History: Additional Questions

There are several other texts from the Deuteronomistic History which might be considered relevant to the focus of this project. These texts have not been analyzed in detail because, with one possible exception, they do not contain explicit references to any sort of *sexual* contact. Since the object of investigation in the present project is an ideological complex having to do with *sexual activity* in its relation to honor, power, and gender (and not, for example, simply gender in its relation to honor and power, which would involve a much wider examination of textual evidence), these other texts have been excluded from the analysis in the previous chapter.

Indeed, if one pursued a detailed investigation of *gender*, honor, and power that included, but did not focus on, the presence of sexual activity (as has this study), one would find a larger range of subject-positions allotted to female characters. For example, such characters as Rahab, Deborah and Jael, Delilah, Michal, Abigail, Jezebel, and Athaliah would need to be discussed, and greater attention would need to be given to the role of the queen mother, mentioned at the end of the previous chapter. Yet explicit references to sexual activity are absent from the tales about most of these women.

Nevertheless, there are points of contact between the focus of the present study and other texts in the Deuteronomistic History. The tales about Samson in the book of Judges, for example, are often considered to have sexual overtones, and it is certainly true that the narratives are constructed in part around Samson's relationships with particular women (cf. Crenshaw 1978). One feature of the stories to which I have already called attention is the characterization of Samson as having long hair which is specifically linked to his strength. We can recall the links that are sometimes made between profuse body hair and virility. It is probably no accident that Samson, defined by his long hair, is frequently seeking women. He is portrayed, culturally speaking, as a 'manly' man.

However, in spite of the recurrence in the Samson narratives of imagery that possibly has sexual overtones (cf. Exum 1993: 77-93), the only reference which seems to be a specific notation of sexual contact in the Samson stories is found in Judg. 16.1, where we are told that Samson saw a prostitute in Gaza and 'went in to her'. The visit may be, in part, a means of characterizing Samson, though it is unclear that there is any attempt to criticize him for sexual misconduct. Rather, Samson's virility is on display, together with an illustration of the fact that he enjoys the company of non-Israelite women.[1] Once again, however, sexual activity is utilized in relation to a situation of conflict between a male character (in this case, Samson) and his enemies, and so is not itself the center of interest in the text. Samson's location inside the city with the prostitute of Gaza functions primarily, within the course of the narrative, to provide an opportunity for the Gazites to attempt to kill him. The woman is, narratologically speaking, an object, and in spite of her qualification as a prostitute she is not represented as having seduced Samson. In these ways she fits into the larger pattern analyzed in this study.

Neither Samson's Philistine wife nor Delilah are portrayed in the text in explicitly sexual situations, although one would not know this from the long tradition of interpretation which has seen Delilah as a sexual seductress. Therefore, the stories about them have not been included in the previous chapter. On the other hand, both of these women do function in terms of relations between male characters, and so fit easily into an interpretation in terms of the male 'traffic in women'. The story of the wife from Timnah is developed around the fact that the Philistine men have, as Samson puts it, 'plowed with my heifer' (Judg. 14.18). While Delilah is given a much larger degree of narrative subjectivity (cf. Bal 1987), her attempts to discover the secret of Samson's strength are framed by references to the Philistines, who both ask her to carry out their request (Judg. 16.5) and, when she has cut Samson's hair, take out his eyes and bring him to Gaza (16.21). Exum has argued that the story of Samson is structured in part around his symbolic emasculation (Exum 1993: 84; cf. Bal 1987: 55).[2] I have argued that some of the other texts considered in this study, and notably the text which recounts Absalom's actions with the concubines of his father, may also be seen as implying a

1.   With reference to this last statement it should be pointed out that, in spite of widespread assumptions to the contrary, it is not actually clear from the texts that Delilah is not an Israelite. See Exum 1993: 69; Frymer-Kensky 1992: 260.

2.   Other texts may be found in the Deuteronomistic History which do not contain references to sexual activity but which do appear to characterize male characters in terms of their failure to embody cultural gender norms and, hence, their symbolic emasculation. What, for example, are we to make of David's curse upon Joab's house that it might never be without someone who holds a 'spindle' or 'distaff' (2 Sam. 3.29)? While the translation of this word is a matter of some disagreement (cf. McCarter 1984: 118), we may have here a curse which hopes for the inclusion, among Joab's male descendants, of men who fail to demonstrate their (culturally defined) masculinity.

sort of symbolic emasculation. Thus, although the stories about Samson differ in certain ways from the stories discussed in Chapter 4, there are intriguing ideological similarities as well.

In addition, quite a number of texts refer, sometimes explicitly, to the phenomenon explored by Rubin in which the exchange of women can mediate relationships between men (cf., for instance, Judg. 3.5-6; 1 Sam. 18.18, 23).[3] I have argued that this phenomenon helps to account for some of the words and actions of the male characters in the texts that mention sexual contact. Further analysis might determine whether and in what ways the 'traffic in women' also helps to account for the structure of texts in which sexual contact as such does not play a role. For example, one could analyze the role of women in the stories about David from this perspective (cf. Linafelt 1992). Such an analysis would highlight the roles played by such female narrative characters as Michal, for Michal is clearly a female character who is utilized in several instances (though not exclusively) in terms of her position in conflicts between male characters (see, for instance, 1 Sam. 18.20-29; 2 Sam. 3.12-16).

Of course, such an analysis could not entirely explain the function of female characters in the David narratives. It would not, for example, account for the significance of those instances in which female characters, through words or deeds, reveal the wisdom or folly of a particular course of action to a male character. Such instances include Abigail's interaction with David (1 Sam. 25.2-42), the words of the Wise Woman of Tekoa (2 Sam. 14.1-20),[4] and Rizpah's attempt to see that the remains of members of the house of Saul are treated honorably (2 Sam. 21.8-14). As a sort of twist on this manner of utilizing female characters, Michal, too, in 2 Sam. 6.16-23, criticizes David for acting in a manner that she considers dishonorable, though it appears that neither David nor the narrator shares her point of view. These texts do give female characters more access to active narrative subject-positions than do the

3.   This phenomenon can have negative connotations. In Judg. 3, for example, the narrator uses the fact that the Israelites give their daughters as wives to the other peoples in the land, and take the daughters of the other peoples as wives, in order to illustrate the fact that, against YHWH's wishes, the Israelites established relationships with those peoples. The text criticizes not the traffic in women per se, but rather the fact that relations were created with particular groups of persons. Cf. Deut. 7.3-4, where religious apostasy is linked with the traffic in women and the resulting relationships.

4.   It should be noted, however, that while the woman of Tekoa is characterized as 'wise', the words she speaks to David are given to her by Joab.

stories about sexual activity analyzed in the previous chapter.

At the same time, even these examples hint at the underlying reality that female characters in the story of David function primarily in texts that focus upon male characters. Three of the four women (Abigail, the woman of Tekoa, and Rizpah) are attempting to intervene in conflicts between male characters, and Abigail, Michal, and Rizpah are themselves caught up in such conflicts at various points in the text. It is in the figure of Tamar, of course, that these various narrative roles come together. On the one hand, Tamar tries to persuade her brother Amnon to take the wiser course of action, while on the other hand, as we have already seen, her brutal treatment turns out to function as a motivation for conflict between male characters. It would seem, then, that the role of female characters in the story of David is too complex to be explained sufficiently by reference *solely* to male struggles for power, but that, indeed, such struggles are one of the major determinants for most narrative figurations of female action and speech.

The Deuteronomistic History also contains some brief manifestations of a particular utilization of sexual imagery which appears in much more detail elsewhere in the Hebrew Bible. In Judg. 2.17, for example, as part of an extended discussion of the continual tendency of the Israelites to abandon exclusive Yahwism, the narrator remarks that the Israelites had illicit intercourse with other gods. The language used here also appears elsewhere in the Deuteronomistic History in this metaphorical sense as a way of referring to the worship of other gods and cultic objects (Judg. 8.27, 33).

This particular sort of sexual rhetoric is actually quite rare in the Deuteronomistic corpus but is utilized much more extensively by such prophets as Jeremiah, Ezekiel, and Hosea (see Weems 1989; 1995; Bird 1989; Yee 1992; Frymer-Kensky 1992). It is more obvious in the latter books that the subject of the sexual unfaithfulness (Israel) is considered to be, as it were, YHWH's wife, and so is to that extent characterized as a woman. Thus, the subject of the sexual unfaithfulness is female, even if this is often only metaphorically the case. The Israelites who are actually being criticized for having worshipped other deities may very well have been male.[5]

---

5. Eilberg-Schwartz has recently attempted to analyze, from a psychoanalytic perspective, the significance of the complicated gender positions involved here: male Israelites visualize themselves as the female spouse of a male deity. For his provocative analysis see Eilberg-Schwartz 1994.

In this regard, the metaphorical use of sexual infidelity differs somewhat from the stories examined in the previous chapter. As we have seen, stories in the Deuteronomistic History which utilize sexual contact in their plots place little emphasis on the role of women as active subjects, particularly with respect to sexual activity. Only the woman in Judges 19 is *possibly* represented as a subject of sexual activity at the beginning of her story, and even this representation (which has little if any impact on the remainder of the story) is based upon a text which can be understood in other ways. Thus, the metaphorical use of sexual activity, which represents Israel as an *actively* unfaithful wife, may rely upon a slightly different ideological position with regard to gender and sexual practice than do the narratives considered in the previous chapter.

The difference between these two positions is in fact reflected in contemporary discussions of the ideologies of sex and gender. Fatima Mernissi has pointed out that female sexuality is sometimes represented as an active and almost insatiable force, which men must constantly strive to control. Hence, in order to avoid the shame that results from the unfaithfulness of their wives, daughters, and sisters, men are admonished to control the women of their household and to restrain them from their sexual impulses (see Mernissi 1987). Carol Delaney, on the other hand, has pointed out, specifically in contrast to the position of Mernissi, that female sexuality is sometimes seen not as insatiable but rather as 'indiscriminate' (Delaney 1987: 41; see also Delaney 1991: 38-42). Delaney argues that, in certain cultures, women are seldom represented as *actively* seeking out illicit sexual relations, but are rather seen, by men at any rate, as having few if any physical or moral defenses against men who might desire such a relationship. Since the women are not considered to be able or willing to protect their own purity against the aggressive sexual impulses that are 'naturally' thought to occur in men, the men of their family must protect it for them. It should be noted that the effect of both of these views of female sexuality (active and insatiable versus passive but indiscriminate) is to offer a justification for the seclusion of women from the public realm of male social intercourse. Both Mernissi and Delaney focus upon cultures from the Mediterranean basin and the Middle East, that part of the world where the dynamics of honor and shame and their relation to female chastity have been studied most thoroughly.[6]

6.   Both scholars discuss the relationship between ideologies of gender and sexuality and the monotheistic religions. This relationship requires further analysis in

One could take the distinct but related views discussed by Mernissi and Delaney and use them as a starting point to compare different bodies of literature within the Hebrew Bible. An initial and admittedly schematic impression is that prophetic books such as Hosea and Ezekiel make use of a perspective which is similar to that discussed by Mernissi, in which female sexuality is considered to be active and insatiable; whereas narrative texts such as those analyzed in Chapter 4 imply a perspective closer to that discussed by Delaney, in which female sexuality is considered to be passive but in need of male protection. In this respect, the imagery found in Judg. 2.17 is actually somewhat closer to the books of Hosea, Ezekiel, and Jeremiah, since Israel's unfaithfulness is portrayed as an active and insatiable one. Both perspectives rely, however, upon a link between male honor and the ability to prevent sexual relationships between another man and the women of one's household. One could also evaluate, in the light of these discussions, the represented relations between women and sexual activity in other narrative traditions such as Genesis, Esther, and Ruth; and in such wisdom traditions as the book of Proverbs.

These considerations may have far-reaching implications. There has been a great deal of discussion in recent years about the fact that the Hebrew Bible uses primarily male imagery and language to speak about YHWH. The issues surrounding these debates have become even more complex now that archaeological evidence has raised at least the possibility that YHWH was in ancient Israel not only a male deity but, in some places at least, a male deity with a female consort (see Olyan 1988; Coogan 1987; McCarter 1987). If YHWH can be represented as a male deity with a female consort, then the gendered language applied to YHWH needs to be interpreted literally, at least insofar as literary, historical, and cultural matters are concerned.[7] The Hebrew Bible, of course, which has primarily been my object of analysis here, is actively opposed to the existence of goddesses as suitable objects of worship for Israelites. Still, in the light of archaeological evidence which implies that YHWH's masculine representation probably needs to be taken literally, the insistence by some literary scholars (see, for instance, Exum 1993; Bal 1988b) that a literary analysis must treat YHWH as a literary character in the company

the case of the Hebrew Bible, particularly in light of important works by Frymer-Kensky (1992) and Eilberg-Schwartz (1994).

7.   The theological significance of this imagery for contemporary readers is, of course, another matter altogether, and lies outside the scope of the present project.

of other literary characters takes on a new meaning. If, as I suggested earlier, gendered characters should be considered in their relation to cultural gender norms, this must hold for the character of YHWH as well.

Hence, the imagery of Israel as YHWH's unfaithful wife may take on specific connotations in a context where the symbolic assumptions discussed in the present project exist. Although the issue cannot be pursued further here, it seems that YHWH may have been represented as a sort of vigilant husband concerned about his masculine honor, who for precisely this reason must prevent illicit sexual relationships between a woman under his authority (Israel) and other potential male sexual partners (such as Baal). Thus, an approach to the biblical texts which takes the ideology of sexual practice in its relation to gender as an explicit point of departure may finally impact our understanding of the characterization of YHWH in the biblical texts, and so also our understanding of biblical theology.

The Question of 'Deuteronomistic' Perspective

The texts analyzed in this study fall within a narrative corpus often referred to as the 'Deuteronomistic History', but these same texts are not themselves generally considered to be part of the specifically 'Deuteronomistic' portions of that corpus. Rather, the stories analyzed here are usually thought to be narrative traditions which were either taken up by the Deuteronomistic Historian(s) or added to the work of the Deuteronomistic Historian(s) at a later time. This fact raises the question of whether we can consider the assumptions about sexual practice analyzed here to be a 'Deuteronomistic' perspective or whether, on the contrary, it might be the case that the concerns about sexual matters which one finds in these texts were not shared, or were not shared in exactly the same way, by the Deuteronomistic Historian(s). Since, in other words, the results of source analysis and tradition history indicate that ideologies, moral values, and so forth can be analyzed in terms of the ways in which they are taken up, modified, recontextualized, and passed on, and since such an analysis would entail a careful consideration of the possible differences in presupposition between earlier traditions and the later frameworks which come to contextualize those traditions,[8] the symbolic assumptions which I have tried to underscore here could be

---

8.   For an analysis of this problem which uses the 'Succession Narrative' as its example, see Knight 1985.

analyzed in terms of the extent to which they are or are not shared by the Deuteronomistic framework into which the stories have been placed.

While a thorough analysis of this question cannot be pursued here, a couple of observations can be made. It is striking that accounts of the lives of narrative figures who are evaluated in a positive or a negative light by the Deuteronomistic Historian(s) do not generally include references to sexual conduct. No mention is made, for example, of the sexual actions of Manasseh as further evidence of his wickedness, or of the sexual actions of Josiah as further evidence of his righteousness. Moreover, when traditions were incorporated into the Deuteronomistic History which already characterized certain figures negatively, no attempt seems to have been made to increase the negative evaluation by casting doubt upon the sexual conduct of the figures in question. The situation is not noticeably different for female characters: neither Jezebel nor Athaliah, for example, is unambiguously characterized in such terms.[9]

How, then, can we account for the difference between the amount of space given over to such questions in the Deuteronomistic History as a whole and the amount of space given to such questions in the 'Succession Narrative' or 'Court History'? The difference may be related to genre. If, for example, the stories about David which comprise the Succession Narrative originated from oral traditions of storytelling, as Gunn argued (1978), rather than, as others (such as von Rad [1984]) have argued, from an eyewitness account of David's court, then one might consider whether the sorts of assumptions analyzed in the present study represent the assumptions of popular folk discourse but not necessarily the interests of the Deuteronomistic Historian(s). Obviously the detailed defense of such a hypothesis would require an examination of such complicated issues as the difference between popular and elite discourse (and specifically whether these two sorts of discourse can be differentiated with respect to assumptions about sexual practice and gender), the ways in which popular discourse is taken up into elite discourse, and the question of whether it is possible today to distinguish folk and elite traditions from

---

9.   The only reference which might conceivably be taken in such a manner is the notation that Jezebel painted her eyes and adorned her hair before meeting Jehu and being thrown out of her window (2 Kgs 9.30). While Jezebel is obviously seen in an extremely negative light, the specifically sexual connotations which even today are often associated with Jezebel in popular discourse (see Pippin 1994) seem generally to postdate the Hebrew Bible.

the ancient world, given the paucity of the evidence.[10] Since one can distinguish a *relative interest* in the effects of sexual contact in the 'Succession Narrative' or 'Court History' from the *relative lack of interest* found elsewhere in its present Deuteronomistic context, such questions deserve further consideration.

From Symbolic Ideology to Social History?

The interpretations offered in the previous chapter focus primarily on literary structures and symbolic, ideological meanings. Although anthropological discussions have been utilized as part of an attempt to contextualize the texts and their cultural presuppositions, the anthropological literature used in this study has primarily come from those streams of cultural anthropology that are focused upon symbolic meanings. Cultural notions rather than social structures or material data have consequently been at the forefront of the preceding discussions. When social structures play a role in the interpretations, it has most often been in reference to their literary representation, and not in relation to a hypothesis about the way things 'really were' in the social world of ancient Israel.

It might therefore seem to some that this study has reproduced, though perhaps in modified form, a tendency toward idealism among scholars of religion in general and biblical scholars in particular. This tendency has been criticized by a number of commentators, including most notably Norman Gottwald (1979; cf. now Gottwald 1993). Such critics point out that the biblical texts were produced in relation to specific social structures and a material context and that this fact needs to be taken more seriously by biblical scholars, who have generally preferred to discuss meanings, great figures, and events. It is therefore worth pointing out that while the analyses presented here have not incorporated material factors to any significant degree, one possible area for future research might be a consideration of the relationship between the symbolic

10. Some of these issues have been discussed in relation to the New Testament by M.A. Tolbert (see, for instance, Tolbert 1989: 59-79). It seems, however, that the methodological problems for the scholar who wishes to examine the Hebrew Bible from such a perspective may be somewhat more difficult, since the amount of non-biblical literature to which appeal might be made in defining 'popular culture' is rather greater for the milieu in which the New Testament was written than for the period in which, it is generally assumed, the Hebrew Bible was written. There is, of course, a long tradition of interpreting parts of the Hebrew Bible in relation to folk discourse (see, for instance, Gunkel 1987).

meanings examined here and such aspects of the social and material history of Israel as are capable of reconstruction on the basis of archaeological and other evidence. Indeed, certain analysts of Mediterranean and Middle Eastern honor and shame have attempted to carry out such an examination (though not specifically in relation to Israel), interpreting male vigilance with regard to female chastity as, in part, a response to the harsh conditions of material scarcity which characterize (and have long characterized) many areas in which the values of honor and shame are particularly stressed (see, for instance, Schneider 1971). A careful consideration of such attempts in relation to descriptions of the social and material world of ancient Israel (by, for instance, Meyers [1988]; Hopkins [1985]) could constitute an important and logical next step for anthropological approaches to biblical literature and the history of Israel, and one toward which the research presented here might contribute.

At the same time, such an attempt would face a number of severe problems so far as the biblical views of sexual practice are concerned. There is no longer any real consensus among biblical scholars about the date of the Deuteronomistic History or its sources. Thus, any attempt to link the ideological complex discussed above too closely with one of the traditional 'periods' of the 'history of Israel' might fail simply on the basis of its inability to justify its choice of historical context. It is precisely for this reason that I have found it preferable to think of context primarily in terms of ideology and frameworks of meaning, rather than in terms of traditional historical periodization.

One possible way of handling this problem, however, might be through the utilization of a less conventional understanding of 'context', such as that provided by the concept of 'mode of production'. 'Mode of production' is a concept which tends to be used by scholars who work with somewhat larger frames of historical periodization than those which biblical scholars, frequently relying upon the biblical narratives, have traditionally employed. David Jobling has recently made a number of helpful suggestions about the possible utilization and extension of the concept of 'mode of production' among biblical scholars (see Jobling 1991a). Significantly, his discussion, which builds not only upon the work of Gottwald (who has called for an analysis by way of the 'mode of production') but also upon the work of several feminist scholars, is centered on the question of gender and touches upon the question of sexual practice, in spite of the fact that both of these questions have tended to be ignored by more traditional Marxist analyses of modes of production. An approach such as that which Jobling begins to lay out in his article may be capable of integrating and building upon the study of the sorts of symbolic meanings analyzed here, and it is possible that such an approach offers one of the best opportunities for carrying out a future integration of symbolic meanings and social and material history.

BIBLIOGRAPHY

Abu-Lughod, L.
1986   *Veiled Sentiments: Honor and Poetry in a Bedouin Society*. Berkeley:
            University of California Press.

Ackerman, J.
1990   'Knowing Good and Evil: A Literary Analysis of the Court History in
            2 Samuel 9–20 and 1 Kings 1–2'. *JBL* 109.1: 41-60.

Ahlström, G.
1986   *Who Were the Israelites?* Winona Lake, IN: Eisenbrauns.

Albright, W.F.
1957   *From the Stone Age to Christianity: Monotheism and the Historical
            Process*. 2nd edn. Baltimore: The Johns Hopkins University Press.
1968   *Yahweh and the Gods of Canaan: A Historical Analysis of Two
            Contrasting Faiths*. London: The Athlone Press.

Alter, R.
1981   *The Art of Biblical Narrative*. New York: Basic Books.
1985   *The Art of Biblical Poetry*. New York: Basic Books.
1989   *The Pleasures of Reading in an Ideological Age*. New York: Simon &
            Schuster.

Antoun, R.
1968   'On the Modesty of Women in Arab Muslim Villages: A Study in the
            Accommodation of Traditions'. *American Anthropologist* 70: 671-97.

Asano-Tamanoi, M.
1987   'Shame, Family, and State in Catalonia and Japan'. In Gilmore (ed.)
            1987: 104-20.

Austin, J.L.
1975   *How To Do Things with Words*. 2nd edn. Cambridge, MA: Harvard
            University Press.

Bailey, R.
1990   *David in Love and War: The Pursuit of Power in 2 Samuel 10–12*.
            JSOTSup, 75. JSOT Press.
1995   'They're Nothing but Incestuous Bastards: The Polemical Use of Sex
            and Sexuality in Hebrew Canon Narratives'. In F. Segovia and M.A.
            Tolbert (eds.), *Reading from this Place: Social Location and Biblical
            Interpretation in the United States*. Minneapolis: Fortress Press: 121-
            38.

Bal, M.
1981a   'Notes on Narrative Embedding'. *Poetics Today* 2.2: 41-59.
1981b   'The Laughing Mice or: On Focalization'. *Poetics Today* 2.2: 202-10.
1983   'The Narrating and the Focalizing: A Theory of the Agents in
            Narrative'. Trans. J.E. Lewin. *Style* 17.2: 234-69.

1985 *Narratology: Introduction to the Theory of Narrative*. Trans. C. van Boheemen. Toronto: University of Toronto Press.

1987 *Lethal Love: Feminist Literary Readings of Biblical Love Stories*. Bloomington: Indiana University Press.

1988a *Murder and Difference: Gender, Genre, and Scholarship on Sisera's Death*. Trans. M. Gumpert. Bloomington: Indiana University Press.

1988b *Death and Dissymmetry: The Politics of Coherence in the Book of Judges*. Chicago: University of Chicago Press.

1989 'Introduction'. In *idem* (ed.), *Anti-Covenant: Counter-Reading Women's Lives in the Hebrew Bible*. Sheffield: Almond Press: 11-24.

1990a 'Dealing/With/Women: Daughters in the Book of Judges'. In R. Schwartz (ed.), *The Book and the Text: The Bible and Literary Theory*. Cambridge: Basil Blackwell: 16-39.

1990b 'The Point of Narratology'. *Poetics Today* 11.4: 727-53.

1990c 'Experiencing Murder: Ritualistic Interpretation of Ancient Texts'. In K. Ashley (ed), *Victor Turner and the Construction of Cultural Criticism: Between Literature and Anthropology*. Bloomington: Indiana University Press: 3-20.

1991a *On Storytelling: Essays in Narratology*. Ed. D. Jobling. Sonoma, CA: Polebridge Press.

1991b *Reading 'Rembrandt': Beyond the Word–Image Opposition*. Cambridge: Cambridge University Press.

1993 'First Person, Second Person, Same Person: Narrative as Epistemology'. *New Literary History* 24: 293-320.

1994 *On Meaning-Making: Essays in Semiotics*. Sonoma, CA: Polebridge Press.

Bal, M., and N. Bryson

1991 'Semiotics and Art History'. *The Art Bulletin* 72.2: 174-208.

Bar-Efrat, S.

1989 *Narrative Art in the Bible*. Sheffield: Almond Press.

Barr, J.

1961 *The Semantics of Biblical Language*. Oxford: Oxford University Press.

1966 *Old and New in Interpretation: A Study of the Two Testaments*. London: SCM Press.

1980 *The Scope and Authority of the Bible*. Philadelphia: Westminster Press.

1987 *Comparative Philology and the Text of the Old Testament*. Repr. Winona Lake, IN: Eisenbrauns. (Original edn, Oxford: Oxford University Press, 1968).

1992 *The Garden of Eden and the Hope of Immortality*. Minneapolis: Fortress Press.

Belsey, C.

1980 *Critical Practice*. London and New York: Routledge.

Berlin, A.

1983 *Poetics and Interpretation of Biblical Narrative*. Sheffield: Almond Press.

Biale, D.

1992 *Eros and the Jews: From Biblical Israel to Contemporary America*. New York: Basic Books.

Bird, P.
   1989   ' "To Play the Harlot": An Inquiry into an Old Testament Metaphor'. In P.L. Day (ed.), *Gender and Difference in Ancient Israel.* Philadelphia: Fortress Press: 75-94.

Blenkinsopp, J.
   1966   'Theme and Motif in the Succession History (2 Sam. XI 2ff.) and the Yahwist Corpus'. In *Volume du Congrès Genève 1965.* VTSup, 15. Leiden: Brill: 44-57.

Blok, A.
   1981   'Rams and Billy-Goats: A Key to the Mediterranean Code of Honour'. *Man* 16: 427-40.

Boling, R.
   1975   *Judges.* AB, 6A. Garden City, NY: Doubleday.

Boswell, J.
   1980   *Christianity, Social Tolerance, and Homosexuality.* Chicago: University of Chicago Press.

Bourdieu, P.
   1977   *Outline of a Theory of Practice.* Cambridge and New York: Cambridge University Press.
   1979   *Algeria 1960.* Cambridge and New York: Cambridge University Press.

Boyarin, D.
   1990   'The Politics of Biblical Narratology: Reading the Bible Like/As a Woman'. *Diacritics* 20.4: 31-42.
   1993   *Carnal Israel: Reading Sex in Talmudic Culture.* The New Historicism: Studies in Cultural Poetics, 25. Berkeley: University of California Press.

Brandes, S.
   1981   'Like Wounded Stags: Male Sexual Ideology in an Andalusian Town'. In Ortner and Whitehead (eds.) 1981: 216-39.
   1987   'Reflections on Honor and Shame in the Mediterranean'. In Gilmore (ed.) 1987: 121-34.

Brenner, A.
   1989   *The Song of Songs.* OTG. Sheffield: JSOT Press.

Brettler, M.
   1989   'The Book of Judges: Literature as Politics'. *JBL* 108.3: 395-418.
   1990   Review of *Murder and Difference* and *Death and Dissymmetry*, by Mieke Bal. *Hebrew Studies* 31: 96-101.

Brooten, B.
   1985   'Paul's Views on the Nature of Women and Female Homoeroticism'. In C. Atkinson, C. Buchanan and M. Miles (eds.), *Immaculate and Powerful: The Female in Sacred Image and Social Reality.* Boston: Beacon Press: 61-87.

Brown, P.
   1988   *The Body and Society: Men, Women, and Sexual Renunciation in Early Christianity.* New York: Columbia University Press.

Bryson, N.
   1992   'Art in Context'. In R. Cohen (ed.), *Studies in Historical Change.* Charlottesville, VA: University of Virginia Press· 18-42.

Burrows, M.
1938   *The Basis of Israelite Marriage.* AOS, 15. New Haven: American
            Oriental Society.
Butler, J.
1990   *Gender Trouble: Feminism and the Subversion of Identity.* New York
            and London: Routledge.
1993   *Bodies That Matter: On the Discursive Limits of 'Sex'.* New York and
            London: Routledge.
Camp, C.
1985   *Wisdom and the Feminine in the Book of Proverbs.* Sheffield: JSOT
            Press.
1991   'Understanding a Patriarchy: Women in Second Century Judaism
            Through the Eyes of Ben Sira'. In A.J. Levine (ed.), *'Women Like
            This': New Perspectives on Jewish Women in the Greco-Roman World.*
            Atlanta: Scholars Press: 1-39.
Campbell, J.K.
1964   *Honour, Family and Patronage.* Oxford: Clarendon Press.
Cantarella, E.
1992   *Bisexuality in the Ancient World.* Trans. C. Culleanáin. New Haven:
            Yale University Press.
Carmichael, C.
1985   *Law and Narrative in the Hebrew Bible: The Evidence of the Deutero-
            nomic Laws and the Decalogue.* Ithaca: Cornell University Press.
Chatman, S.
1978   *Story and Discourse: Narrative Structure in Fiction and Film.* Ithaca:
            Cornell University Press.
Clifford, J.
1988   *The Predicament of Culture: Twentieth-Century Ethnography,
            Literature, and Art.* Cambridge, MA: Harvard University Press.
Clifford, J., and G.E. Marcus (eds.)
1986   *Writing Culture: The Poetics and Politics of Ethnography.* Berkeley:
            University of California Press.
Conroy, C.
1978   *Absalom Absalom! Narrative and Language in 2 Sam 13–20.* Rome:
            Biblical Institute Press.
Coogan, M.D.
1987   'Canaanite Origins and Lineage: Reflections on the Religion of
            Ancient Israel'. In P.D. Miller, Jr, P.D. Hanson and S.D. McBride
            (eds.), *Ancient Israelite Religion: Essays in Honor of Frank Moore
            Cross.* Philadelphia: Fortress Press: 115-24.
Coote, R., and K. Whitelam
1987   *The Emergence of Early Israel in Historical Perspective.* The Social
            World of Biblical Antiquity. Sheffield: Almond Press.
Crenshaw, J.
1978   *Samson: A Secret Betrayed, A Vow Ignored.* Atlanta: John Knox Press.
Cross, F.M.
1973   *Canaanite Myth and Hebrew Epic: Essays on the History of the
            Religion of Israel.* Cambridge, MA: Harvard University Press.

Culler, J.
  1975   *Structuralist Poetics: Structuralism, Linguistics, and the Study of Literature*. Ithaca: Cornell University Press.
  1981   *The Pursuit of Signs: Semiotics, Literature, Deconstruction*. Ithaca: Cornell University Press.
  1982   *On Deconstruction: Theory and Criticism after Structuralism*. Ithaca: Cornell University Press.
  1988   *Framing the Sign: Criticism and its Institutions*. Norman: University of Oklahoma Press.
Culley, R.C.
  1976   *Studies in the Structure of Hebrew Narrative*. Missoula, MT: Scholars Press.
Culpepper, R.A.
  1983   *Anatomy of the Fourth Gospel: A Study in Literary Design*. Philadelphia: Fortress Press.
Davies, P.R.
  1992   *In Search of 'Ancient Israel'*. JSOTSup, 148. Sheffield: JSOT Press.
Davis, J.
  1977   *People of the Mediterranean*. London: Routledge & Kegan Paul.
  1987   'Family and State in the Mediterranean'. In Gilmore (ed.) 1987: 22-34.
Day, P.L.
  1989   'From the Child is Born the Woman: The Story of Jephthah's Daughter'. In *idem* (ed.), *Gender and Difference in Ancient Israel*. Minneapolis: Fortress Press: 58-74.
  1991   'Why is Anat a Warrior and a Hunter?' In D. Jobling, P.L. Day and G.T. Sheppard (eds.), *The Bible and the Politics of Exegesis*. Cleveland: The Pilgrim Press: 141-46.
Delaney, C.
  1987   'Seeds of Honor, Fields of Shame'. In Gilmore (ed.) 1987: 35-48.
  1991   *The Seed and the Soil: Gender and Cosmology in Turkish Village Society*. Berkeley: University of California Press: 35-48.
Dever, W.G.
  1990   *Recent Archaeological Discoveries and Biblical Research*. Seattle: University of Washington Press.
Dietrich, W.
  1972   *Prophetie und Geschichte: Eine redaktionsgeschichtliche Untersuchung zum deuteronomistischen Geschichtswerk*. FRLANT, 108. Göttingen: Vandenhoeck & Ruprecht.
Douglas, M.
  1966   *Purity and Danger: An Analysis of the Concepts of Pollution and Taboo*. London: Routledge.
  1975   *Implicit Meanings*. Boston: Routledge & Kegan Paul.
Dover, K.
  1989 [1978] *Greek Homosexuality*. 2nd edn. Cambridge, MA: Harvard University Press.
Eagleton, T.
  1991   *Ideology: An Introduction*. London and New York: Verso.

Eilberg-Schwartz, H.
    1990   *The Savage in Judaism: An Anthropology of Israelite Religion and Ancient Judaism.* Bloomington: Indiana University Press.
    1994   *God's Phallus and Other Problems for Men and Monotheism.* Boston: Beacon Press.
Eilberg Schwartz, H. (ed.)
    1992   *People of the Body: Jews and Judaism from an Embodied Perspective.* Albany: The State University of New York Press.
Exum, J.C.
    1993   *Fragmented Women: Feminist (Sub)Versions of Biblical Narratives.* Valley Forge, PA: Trinity Press International.
Fabian, J.
    1983   *Time and the Other: How Anthropology Makes its Object.* New York: Columbia University Press.
Falk, M.
    1982   *Love Lyrics from the Bible: A Translation and Literary Study of the Song of Songs.* Sheffield: Almond Press.
Fewell, D.N., and D. Gunn
    1993   *Gender, Power, and Promise: The Subject of the Bible's First Story.* Nashville: Abingdon Press.
Finley, M.I.
    1978   *The World of Odysseus.* 2nd edn. New York: Penguin Books.
Flanagan, J. W.
    1988 [1972] *David's Social Drama: A Hologram of Israel's Early Iron Age.* The Social World of Biblical Antiquity. Sheffield: Almond Press.
Fokkelman, J.P.
    1981   *King David (II Sam. 9.20 & I Kings 1–2).* Assen: Van Gorcum.
Foucault, M.
    1978   *The History of Sexuality. Volume I: An Introduction.* Trans. R. Hurley. New York: Random House.
    1980   *Power/Knowledge: Selected Interviews and Other Writings: 1972– 1977.* Ed. C. Gordon. New York: Pantheon.
    1985   *The Use of Pleasure.* Trans. R. Hurley. New York: Random House.
    1986   *The Care of the Self.* Trans. R. Hurley. New York: Random House.
Friedman, R.E.
    1981   *The Exile and Biblical Narrative.* Chico, CA: Scholars Press.
Frymer-Kensky, T.
    1989   'Law and Philosophy: The Case of Sex in the Bible'. *Semeia* 44: 89- 102.
    1992   *In the Wake of the Goddesses: Women, Culture, and the Biblical Transformation of Pagan Myth.* New York: Free Press.
Fuchs, E.
    1985   'The Literary Characterization of Mothers and Sexual Politics in the Hebrew Bible'. In A.Y. Collins (ed.), *Feminist Perspectives on Biblical Scholarship.* Chico, CA: Scholars Press: 117-36 .
Fuller, R.
    1993   'Adultery'. In B.M. Metzger and M.D. Coogan (eds.), *The Oxford*

Companion to the Bible. New York and Oxford: Oxford University Press: 10.

Gadamer, H.G.
1985 [1960] *Truth and Method*. 2nd edn. New York: Crossroad.

Garbini, G.
1988 *History and Ideology in Ancient Israel*. Trans. J. Bowden. New York: Crossroad.

Geertz, C.
1973 *The Interpretation of Cultures*. New York: Basic Books.
1983 *Local Knowledge: Further Essays in Interpretive Anthropology*. New York: Basic Books.
1988 *Works and Lives: The Anthropologist as Author*. Stanford, CA: Stanford University Press.

Genette, G.
1980 *Narrative Discourse: An Essay in Method*. Trans. J. Lewin. Ithaca: Cornell University Press.

Gilmore, D.
1987a 'Introduction: The Shame of Dishonor'. In Gilmore (ed.) 1987: 2-21.
1987b 'Honor, Honesty, Shame: Male Status in Contemporary Andalusia'. In Gilmore (ed.) 1987: 90-103.
1990 *Manhood in the Making: Cultural Concepts of Masculinity*. New Haven: Yale University Press.

Gilmore, D. (ed.)
1987 *Honor and Shame and the Unity of the Mediterranean*. Washington, DC: American Anthropological Association.

Giovannini, M.
1981 'Woman: A Dominant Symbol within the Cultural System of a Sicilian Town'. *Man* 16: 408-26.
1987 'Female Chastity Codes in the Circum-Mediterranean: Comparative Perspectives'. In Gilmore (ed.) 1987: 61-74.

Gleason, M.
1990 'The Semiotics of Gender: Physiognomy and Self-Fashioning in the Second Century CE'. In Halperin, Winkler and Zeitlin (eds.) 1990: 389-415.

Goddard, V.
1987 'Honour and Shame: The Control of Women's Sexuality and Group Identity in Naples'. In P. Caplan (ed.), *The Cultural Construction of Sexuality*. London and New York: Tavistock Publications: 166-92.

Gottwald, N.
1979 *The Tribes of Yahweh: A Sociology of the Religion of Liberated Israel, 1250–1050 BCE*. Maryknoll, NY: Orbis Books.
1985 *The Hebrew Bible: A Socio-Literary Introduction*. Philadelphia: Fortress Press.
1993 *The Hebrew Bible in its Social World and in Ours*. Atlanta: Scholars Press.

Gottwald, N. (ed.)
1986 *Social Scientific Criticism of the Hebrew Bible and its Social World: The Israelite Monarchy. Semeia*, 37. Atlanta: Scholars Press.

Gouldner, A.
1965   *Enter Plato: Classical Greece and the Origins of Social Theory.* New York: Basic Books.
Gray, J.
1963   *I & II Kings: A Commentary.* Philadelphia: Westminster Press.
Greenberg, D.F.
1988   *The Construction of Homosexuality.* Chicago: University of Chicago Press.
Gunkel, H.
1987   *The Folktale in the Old Testament.* Trans. M. Rutter. Ed. D. Gunn. Sheffield: Almond Press.
Gunn, D.
1978   *The Story of King David: Genre and Interpretation.* JSOTSup, 6. Sheffield: JSOT Press.
Hackett, J.A.
1992   '1 and 2 Samuel'. In C. Newsom and S. Ringe (eds.), *The Women's Bible Commentary.* Louisville, KY: Westminster/John Knox Press: 85-95.
Hall, E.
1976   *Beyond Culture.* Garden City, NY: Doubleday.
Halperin, D.
1990   *One Hundred Years of Homosexuality and Other Essays on Greek Love.* New York: Routledge.
Halperin, D., J. Winkler and F. Zeitlin (eds.)
1990   *Before Sexuality: The Construction of Erotic Experience in the Ancient Greek World.* Princeton: Princeton University Press.
Halpern, B.
1988   *The First Historians: The Hebrew Bible and History.* San Francisco: Harper & Row.
Hertzberg, H.
1964   *I & II Samuel.* OTL. Philadelphia: Westminster Press.
Herzfeld, M.
1985   *The Poetics of Manhood: Contest and Identity in a Cretan Mountain Village.* Princeton: Princeton University Press.
1987   '"As in Your Own House": Hospitality, Ethnography, and the Stereotype of Mediterranean Society'. In Gilmore (ed.) 1987: 75-89.
Hillers, D.
1985   'Analyzing the Abominable: Our Understanding of Canaanite Religion'. *JQR* 75.3: 253-69.
Hopkins, D.
1985   *The Highlands of Canaan: Agricultural Life in the Early Iron Age.* The Social World of Biblical Antiquity. Sheffield: Almond Press.
Holy, L.
1989   *Kinship, Honour and Solidarity: Cousin Marriage in the Middle East.* Manchester and New York: Manchester University Press.
Hunt, L. (ed.)
1989   *The New Cultural History.* Berkeley: University of California Press.

Ishida, T.
1977   *The Royal Dynasties in Ancient Israel.* Berlin: de Gruyter.
Jameson, F.
1981   *The Political Unconscious: Narrative as a Socially Symbolic Act.*
            Ithaca: Cornell University Press.
Jamieson-Drake, D.W.
1991   *Scribes and Schools in Monarchic Judah: A Socio-Archeological
            Approach.* The Social World of Biblical Antiquity, 9. Sheffield:
            Almond Press.
Jobling, D.
1990   'Writing the Wrongs of the World: The Deconstruction of the Biblical
            Text in the Context of Liberation Theologies'. *Semeia* 51: 81-118.
1991a   'Feminism and "Mode of Production" in Ancient Israel: Search for a
            Method'. In D. Jobling, P.L. Day and G.T. Sheppard (eds.), *The Bible
            and the Politics of Exegesis.* Cleveland: Pilgrim Press: 239-51.
1991b   'Mieke Bal on Biblical Narrative'. *RelSRev* 17: 1-10.
Keefe, A.
1993   'Rapes of Women/Wars of Men'. *Semeia* 61: 79-97.
Keuls, E.
1985   *The Reign of the Phallus: Sexual Politics in Ancient Athens.* Berkeley:
            University of California Press.
Knight, D.
1985   'Moral Values and Literary Traditions: The Case of the Succession
            Narrative (2 Samuel 9–20; 1 Kings 1–2). *Semeia* 34: 7-135.
Lancaster, R.N.
1988   'Subject Honor and Object Shame: The Construction of Male
            Homosexuality and Stigma in Nicaragua'. *Ethnology* 27: 111-25.
1992   *Life is Hard: Machismo, Danger, and the Intimacy of Power in
            Nicaragua.* Berkeley: University of California Press.
Lang, B. (ed.)
1985   *Anthropological Approaches to the Old Testament.* Issues in Religion
            and Theology, 8. London: SPCK; Philadelphia: Fortress Press.
Laqueur, T.
1990   *Making Sex: Body and Gender from the Greeks to Freud.* Cambridge,
            MA: Harvard University Press.
Lasine, S.
1984   'Guest and Host in Judges 19: Lot's Hospitality in an Inverted World'.
            JSOT 29: 37-59.
Leach, E.
1969   *Genesis as Myth and Other Essays.* London: Jonathan Cape.
1982   'Anthropological Approaches to the Study of the Bible during the
            Twentieth Century'. In G. Tucker and D.A. Knight (eds.), *Humanizing
            America's Iconic Book: Society of Biblical Literature Centennial
            Addresses 1980.* Chico, CA: Scholars Press: 73-94.
Leick, G.
1994   *Sex and Eroticism in Mesopotamian Literature.* London and New
            York: Routledge.

Leith, M.
1993   'Samson'. In B.M. Metzger and M.D. Coogan (eds.), *The Oxford Companion to the Bible*. New York: Oxford University Press: 673.
Lemche, N.P.
1985   *Early Israel: Anthropological and Historical Studies on the Israelite Society Before the Monarchy*. VTSup, 37. Leiden: Brill.
1988   *Ancient Israel: A New History of Israelite Society*. The Biblical Seminar. Sheffield: JSOT Press.
1991   *The Canaanites and their Land*. JSOTSup, 110. Sheffield: JSOT Press.
Levenson, J.
1978   'I Samuel 25 as Literature and History'. *CBQ* 40: 11-28.
Levenson, J., and B. Halpern
1980   'The Political Import of David's Marriages'. *JBL* 99: 507-18.
Lévi-Strauss, C.
1969   *The Elementary Structures of Kinship*. Boston: Beacon Press.
Lichtheim, M.
1976   *Ancient Egyptian Literature*. II. *The New Kingdom*. Berkeley: University of California Press.
Linafelt, T.
1992   'Taking Women in Samuel: Readers/Responses/Responsibility'. In D.N. Fewell (ed.), *Reading Between Texts: Intertextuality and the Hebrew Bible*. Philadelphia: Westminster Press: 99-113.
Lindisfarne, N.
1994   'Variant Masculinities, Variant Virginities: Rethinking "Honour and Shame."' In A. Cornwall and N. Lindisfarne (eds.), *Dislocating Masculinity: Comparative Ethnographies*. London and New York: Routledge: 82-96.
Liverani, M.
1979   *Three Amarna Essays*. Trans. M.L. Jaffe. Sources and Monographs on the Ancient Near East. Malibu: Undena Publications.
Malina, B.
1981   *The New Testament: Insights from Cultural Anthropology*. Louisville, KY: John Knox Press.
1991a   'Interpretation: Reading, Abduction, Metaphor'. In D. Jobling, P.L. Day and G.T. Sheppard (eds.), *The Bible and the Politics of Exegesis*. Cleveland: The Pilgrim Press: 253-66.
1991b   'Reading Theory Perspective: Reading Luke–Acts'. In Neyrey (ed.) 1991: 3-23.
Marcus, M.A.
1987   '"Horsemen are the Fence of the Land": Honor and History Among the Ghiyata of Eastern Morocco'. In Gilmore (ed.) 1987: 49-60.
Martin, D.B.
1993   'Social-Scientific Criticism'. In S.L. McKenzie and S.R. Haynes (eds.), *To Each its Own Meaning: An Introduction to Biblical Criticisms and their Application*. Louisville, KY: Westminster/John Knox Press: 103-19.

Martin, W.
    1986   *Recent Theories of Narrative*. Ithaca and London: Cornell University Press.
Matejka, L., and K. Pomorska (eds.)
    1971   *Readings in Russian Poetics*. Cambridge, MA: The MIT Press.
Matthews, V.
    1992   'Hospitality and Hostility in Genesis 19 and Judges 19'. *BTB* 22.1: 3-11.
Matthews, V., and D. Benjamin (eds.)
    1993   *Social World of Ancient Israel, 1250–587 BCE*. Peabody, MA: Hendrickson.
Mauss, M.
    1990   *The Gift*. Trans. W.D. Halls. New York: W.W. Norton.
Mayes, A.D.H.
    1974   *Israel in the Period of the Judges*. London: SCM Press.
    1983   *The Story of Israel between Settlement and Exile*. London: SCM Press.
McCarter, P.K.
    1980   *I Samuel*. AB, 8. Garden City, NY: Doubleday.
    1984   *II Samuel*. AB, 9. Garden City, NY: Doubleday.
    1987   'Aspects of the Religion of the Israelite Monarchy: Biblical and Epigraphic Data'. In P.D. Miller, Jr, P.D. Hanson and S.D. McBride (eds.), *Ancient Israelite Religion: Essays in Honor of Frank Moore Cross*. Philadelphia: Fortress Press: 137-55.
McNutt, P.
    1990   *The Forging of Israel: Iron Technology, Symbolism, and Tradition in Ancient Society*. The Social World of Biblical Antiquity. Sheffield: Almond Press.
Meijer, M.
    1993   'Countering Textual Violence: On the Critique of Representation and the Importance of Teaching its Methods'. *Women's Studies International Forum* 16.4: 367-78.
Mernissi, F.
    1987   *Beyond the Veil: Male–Female Dynamics in Modern Muslim Society*. Rev. edn. Bloomington and Indianapolis: Indiana University Press.
Meyers, C.
    1988   *Discovering Eve: Ancient Israelite Women in Context*. New York: Oxford University Press.
Mitchell, J.
    1974   *Psychoanalysis and Feminism*. New York: Random House.
Moore, H.
    1988   *Feminism and Anthropology*. Minneapolis: University of Minnesota Press.
Mullen, E.T., Jr
    1993   *Narrative History and Ethnic Boundaries: The Deuteronomistic History and the Creation of Israelite National Identity*. Semeia Studies. Atlanta: Scholars Press.

Nelson, R.
1981   *The Double Redaction of the Deuteronomistic History*. JSOTSup, 18.
            Sheffield: JSOT Press.
Neyrey, J. (ed.)
1991   *The Social World of Luke–Acts: Models for Interpretation*. Peabody,
            MA: Hendrickson.
Niditch, S.
1982   'The "Sodomite" Theme in Judges 19–20: Family, Community, and
            Social Disintegration'. *CBQ* 44: 365-78.
1993   *War in the Hebrew Bible: A Study in the Ethics of Violence*. New York:
            Oxford University Press.
Nieuwenhuijze, C.A.O.
1971   *Sociology of the Middle East: A Stocktaking and Interpretation*. Social,
            Economic, and Political Studies of the Middle East, 1. Leiden: Brill.
Noth, M.
1930   *Das System der zwölf Stämme Israels*. Stuttgart: Kohlhammer.
1960 [1954] *The History of Israel*. Rev edn. New York: Harper & Row.
1991 [1943] *The Deuteronomistic History*. 2nd edn. JSOTSup, 15. Sheffield: JSOT
            Press.
Oden, R.
1987   *The Bible Without Theology*. San Francisco: Harper & Row.
Olyan, S.M.
1988   *Asherah and the Cult of Yahweh in Israel*. SBLMS, 34. Atlanta:
            Scholars Press.
1994   '"And with a Male You Shall Not Lie the Lying Down of a Woman":
            On the Meaning and Significance of Leviticus 18.22 and 20.13'.
            Journal of the History of Sexuality 5.2: 179-206.
Ortner, S.B.
1978   'The Virgin and the State'. *Feminist Studies* 4: 19-33.
Ortner, S.B., and H. Whitehead
1981   'Introduction: Accounting for Sexual Meanings'. In Ortner and
            Whitehead (eds.) 1981: 1-27.
Ortner, S.B., and H. Whitehead (eds.)
1981   *Sexual Meanings: The Cultural Construction of Gender and Sexuality*.
            Cambridge and New York: Cambridge University Press.
Padgug, R.
1989 [1979] 'Sexual Matters: On Conceptualizing Sexuality in History'. In K. Peiss
            and C. Simmons (eds.), *Passion and Power: Sexuality in History*.
            Philadelphia: Temple University Press: 14-31.
Parker, S.
1991   'The Hebrew Bible and Homosexuality'. *Quarterly Review* 11.3: 4-19.
Patai, R.
1959   *Sex and Family in the Bible and the Middle East*. Garden City, NY:
            Doubleday.
Penchansky, D.
1992   'Staying the Night: Intertextuality in Genesis and Judges'. In D.N.
            Fewell (ed.), *Reading Between Texts: Intertextuality and the Hebrew
            Bible*. Louisville, KY: Westminster/John Knox Press: 77-88.

Peristiany, J.G. (ed.)
1965   *Honour and Shame: The Values of Mediterranean Society.* London:
            Weidenfeld & Nicolson.
Pippin, T.
1994   'Jezebel Re-Vamped'. In A. Brenner (ed.), *A Feminist Companion to
            Samuel and Kings.* The Feminist Companion to the Bible, 5. Sheffield:
            Sheffield Academic Press: 196-206.
Pitt-Rivers, J.
1977   *The Fate of Shechem or the Politics of Sex.* Cambridge: Cambridge
            University Press.
Polzin, R.
1989   *Samuel and the Deuteronomist: A Literary Study of the Deuteronomistic
            History.* San Francisco: Harper & Row.
Pope, M.
1977   *Song of Songs.* AB, 7c. Garden City, NY: Doubleday.
Prince, G.
1982   *Narratology: The Form and Function of Narrative.* Berlin: Mouton.
1988   'Narratological Illustrations'. *Semiotica* 68.3/4: 355-66.
Rad, G. von.
1984 [1966] *The Problem of the Hexateuch and Other Essays.* Trans. E.W. Trueman
            Dicken. London: SCM Press.
Richlin, A.
1993   'Not Before Homosexuality: The Materiality of the *Cinaedus* and the
            Roman Law against Love between Men'. *Journal of the History of
            Sexuality* 3.4: 523-73.
Richter, H.F.
1978   *Geschlechtlichkeit, Ehe und Familie im Alten Testament und seiner
            Umwelt.* Beiträge zur biblischen Exegese und Theologie. Frankfurt am
            Main: Peter Lang.
Ricoeur, P.
1981   *Hermeneutics and the Human Sciences.* Trans. and ed. J.B. Thompson.
            Cambridge: Cambridge University Press.
Rimmon-Kenan, S.
1983   *Narrative Fiction: Contemporary Poetics.* London: Methuen.
Rogerson, J.W.
1984 [1978] *Anthropology and the Old Testament.* The Biblical Seminar, 1.
            Sheffield: JSOT Press.
1989   'Anthropology and the Old Testament'. In R.E. Clements (ed.), *The
            World of Ancient Israel: Sociological, Anthropological and Political
            Perspectives.* Cambridge: Cambridge University Press: 17-37.
Rosaldo, R.
1989   *Culture and Truth: The Remaking of Social Analysis.* Boston: Beacon
            Press.
Rost, L.
1982 [1926] *The Succession to the Throne of David.* Trans. E. Ball. Sheffield:
            Almond Press.

Rousselle, A.
1988 [1983] *Porneia: On Desire and the Body in Antiquity*. Trans. F. Pheasant.
Oxford and New York: Basil Blackwell.

Rubin, G.
1975 'The Traffic in Women: Notes on the "Political Economy" of Sex'.
In R. Reiter (ed.), *Toward an Anthropology of Women*. New York:
Monthly Review Press: 157-210.
1984 'Thinking Sex: Notes for a Radical Theory of the Politics of Sexuality'.
In C. Vance (ed.), *Pleasure and Danger: Exploring Female Sexuality*.
Boston and London: Routledge & Kegan Paul: 267-319.

Sahlins, M.
1972 *Stone Age Economics*. New York: Aldine/de Gruyter.

Schneider, J.
1971 'Of Vigilance and Virgins: Honor, Shame and Access to Resources in
Mediterranean Societies'. *Ethnology* 10.1: 1-24.

Schwartz, R.
1991 'Adultery in the House of David: The Metanarrative of Biblical
Scholarship and the Narratives of the Bible'. *Semeia* 54: 35-55.

Sedgwick, E.
1985 *Between Men: English Literature and Male Homosocial Desire*. New
York: Columbia University Press.

Segovia, F.
1995 '"And They Began to Speak in Other Tongues": Competing Modes
of Discourse in Contemporary Biblical Criticism'. In F. Segovia and
M.A. Tolbert (eds.), *Reading From This Place*. I. *Social Location and
Biblical Interpretation in the United States*. Minneapolis: Fortress
Press: 1-32.

Simkins, R.
1994 *Creator and Creation: Nature in the Worldview of Ancient Israel*.
Peabody, MA: Hendrickson.

Smend, R.
1971 'Das Gesetz und die Völker: Ein Beitrag zur deuteronomistischen
Redaktionsgeschichte'. In H.W. Wolff (ed.), *Probleme biblischer
Theologie: Gerhard von Rad zum 70. Geburtstag*. Munich: Chr.
Kaiser Verlag: 494-509.

Smith, M.
1987 [1971] *Palestinian Parties and Politics that Shaped the Old Testament*.
London: SCM Press.

Soggin, J.A.
1981 *Judges: A Commentary*. OTL. Philadelphia: Westminster Press.
1989 *Introduction to the Old Testament*. OTL. 3rd edn. Philadelphia:
Westminster Press.

Steinberg, N.
1993 *Kinship and Marriage in Genesis: A Household Economics
Perspective*. Minneapolis: Fortress Press.

Sternberg, M.
1985 *The Poetics of Biblical Narrative: Ideological Literature and the
Drama of Reading*. Bloomington: Indiana University Press.

Suleiman, S., and I. Crosman (eds.)
  1980   *The Reader in the Text: Essays on Audience and Interpretation.* Princeton: Princeton University Press.

Talmon, S.
  1978   'The "Comparative Method" in Biblical Interpretation—Principles and Problems'. In *Congress Volume Göttingen 1977*. VTSup, 29. Leiden: Brill: 320-56.
  1986   *King, Cult and Calendar in Ancient Israel.* Jerusalem: Magnes Press.

Tapper, N.
  1991   *Bartered Brides: Politics, Gender and Marriage in an Afghan Tribal Society.* Cambridge and New York: Cambridge University Press.

Todorov, T.
  1977   *The Poetics of Prose.* Trans. R. Howard. Ithaca: Cornell University Press.

Tolbert, M.A.
  1989   *Sowing the Gospel: Mark's World in Literary-Historical Perspective.* Minneapolis: Fortress Press.
  1993   'Social, Sociological, and Anthropological Methods'. In E. Schüssler Fiorenza (ed.), *Searching the Scriptures. I. A Feminist Introduction.* New York: Crossroad: 255-71.

Tompkins, J. (ed.)
  1980   *Reader-Response Criticism: From Formalism to Post-Structuralism.* Baltimore: Johns Hopkins University Press.

Toolan, M.
  1988   *Narrative: A Critical Linguistic Introduction.* London and New York: Routledge.

Trible, P.
  1984   *Texts of Terror: Literary-Feminist Readings of Biblical Narratives.* Overtures to Biblical Theology. Philadelphia: Fortress Press.

Tsevat, M.
  1958   'Marriage and Monarchical Legitimacy in Ugarit and Israel'. *JSS* 3: 237-43.
  1977   'בתולה *bethulah*; בתולים *bethulim*'. In *TDOT*, II: 338-43.

Van Der Horst, P.W.
  1985   'Pseudo-Phocylides: A New Translation and Introduction'. In J.H. Charlesworth (ed.), *The Old Testament Pseudepigrapha.* Garden City, NY: Doubleday: 565-82.

Van Dijk-Hemmes, F.
  1989   'Tamar and the Limits of Patriarchy: Between Rape and Seduction'. In M. Bal (ed.), *Anti-Covenant: Counter-Reading Women's Lives in the Hebrew Bible.* Sheffield: Almond Press: 135-56.

Van Seters, J.
  1983   *In Search of History: Historiography in the Ancient World and the Origins of Biblical History.* New Haven: Yale University Press.
  1987   'Love and Death in the Court History of David'. In J. Marks and R. Good (eds.), *Love and Death in the Ancient Near East: Essays in Honor of Marvin H. Pope.* Guilford, CT: Four Quarters Publishing: 121-24.

Veeser, H.A. (ed.)
1989   *The New Historicism*. New York: Routledge.
Veijola, T.
1975   *Die Ewige Dynastie: David und die Entstehung seiner Dynastie nach der deuteronomistischen Darstellung*. Helsinki: Academia Scientiarum Fennica.
1977   *Das Königtum in der Beurteilung der deuteronomistischen Historiographie: Eine redaktionsgeschichtliche Untersuchung*. Helsinki: Academia Scientarum Fennica.
Veyne, P.
1985   'Homosexuality in Ancient Rome'. In P. Ariès and A. Béjin (eds.), *Western Sexuality: Practice and Precept in Past and Present Times*. Trans. A. Forster. Oxford and New York: Basil Blackwell: 26-35.
Weeks, J.
1985   *Sexuality and its Discontents: Meanings, Myths and Modern Sexualities*. London, Boston and Henley: Routlege & Kegan Paul.
Weems, R.J.
1989   'Gomer: Victim of Violence or Victim of Metaphor'. *Semeia* 47: 87-104.
1992   'The Hebrew Women are Not Like the Egyptian Women: The Ideology of Race, Gender and Sexual Reproduction in Exodus 1'. *Semeia* 59: 25-34.
1995   *Battered Love: Marriage, Sex, and Violence in the Hebrew Prophets*. Overtures to Biblical Theology. Minneapolis: Fortress Press.
Wellhausen, J.
1957 [1878] *Prolegomena to the History of Ancient Israel*. New York: Meridian Books.
Wenham, G.J.
1972   '*Betulah*: A Girl of Marriageable Age'. *VT* 22: 326-48.
Whybray, R.N.
1968   *The Succession Narrative*. London: SCM Press.
White, H.
1973   *Metahistory: The Historical Imagination in Nineteenth-Century Europe*. Baltimore: Johns Hopkins University Press.
1978   *Tropics of Discourse: Essays in Cultural Criticism*. Baltimore: Johns Hopkins University Press.
1987   *The Content of the Form: Narrative Discourse and Historical Representation*. Baltimore: Johns Hopkins University Press.
Wikan, U.
1984   'Shame and Honour: A Contestable Pair'. *Man* 19: 635-52.
1991 [1982] *Behind the Veil in Arabia*. Chicago: University of Chicago Press.
Wilson, R.
1977   *Genealogy and History in the Biblical World*. New Haven: Yale University Press.
1980   *Prophecy and Society in Ancient Israel*. Philadelphia: Fortress Press.
1984   *Sociological Approaches to the Old Testament*. Guides to Biblical Scholarship. Philadelphia: Fortress Press.

Winkler, J.J.
  1990   *The Constraints of Desire: The Anthropology of Sex and Gender in Ancient Greece.* New York: Routledge.

Wolff, H.W.
  1974   *Hosea: A Commentary on the Book of the Prophet Hosea.* Hermeneia. Trans. G. Stansell. Ed. P.D. Hanson. Philadelphia: Fortress Press.
  1977   *Joel and Amos: A Commentary on the Books of the Prophets Joel and Amos.* Hermeneia. Trans. W. Janzen, S.D. McBride, Jr, and C. Muenchow. Ed. S.D. McBride, Jr. Philadelphia: Fortress Press.

Wright, R.A.
  1989   'Establishing Hospitality in the Old Testament: Testing the Tool of Linguistic Pragmatics'. PhD dissertation, Yale University.

Yee, G.
  1992   'Hosea'. In C. Newsom and S. Ringe (eds.), *The Women's Bible Commentary.* Louisville, KY: Westminster/John Knox Press: 195-202.

Young, I.M.
  1990   *Throwing Like a Girl and Other Essays in Feminist Philosophy and Social Theory.* Bloomington and Indianapolis: Indiana University Press.

INDEXES

INDEX OF REFERENCES

OLD TESTAMENT

INDEX OF AUTHORS

JOURNAL FOR THE STUDY OF THE OLD TESTAMENT
SUPPLEMENT SERIES